The Evolution of Integral Consciousness

D1596403

Cover art by JANE EVANS

ABOUT THE AUTHOR

Haridas Chaudhuri was born in May of 1913, in Shyama-gram, East Bengal. Although orphaned at an early age, he was self-directed towards meaningful achievements. In 1929, he won the Ramtanu Gold Medal in Bengali literature when he graduated from high school. He went on to receive his B.A. and M.A. with honors in Philosophy and Religion from the Vidyasagar College in Calcutta. There he received the Gold Medal for highest scholastic achievement, as well as the Silver Medal from his Department. In 1949, he received his Ph.D. from the University of Calcutta for the dissertation, "Integral Idealism". Dr. Chaudhuri then became a member of the educational service of the Government of West Bengal and chairman of the department of philosophy at Krishnager College.

In 1951, Dr. Chaudhuri came to the United States at the nomination of the great Indian sage, Sri Aurobindo, and at the invitation of Dr. Frederic Spiegelberg of Stanford University to teach at the American Academy of Asian Studies. From this experience, he went on to become the founder of the Cutlural Integration Fellowship, dedicated to the promotion of intercultural understanding between East and West, and Director of the Center of Universal Religion, in San Francisco. Further, he founded and served as President (as well as Professor of Philosophy) at the California Institute of Asian Studies, which offers graduate degrees in Philosophy, Psychology, Asian Area, and Integral-Interdisciplinary Studies.

Dr. Chaudhuri wrote and published more than a dozen books, some fifty articles, and lectured widely around the world. He was a member of the American Philosophical Association and the American Oriental Society.

He passed on in June of 1975, leaving the world with treasures to be discovered and used within the philosophical wisdom he embodied and conveyed.

The Evolution of Integral Consciousness

by Haridas Chaudhuri

*Founder of the California Institute
of Asian Studies*

 A
QUEST BOOK

*This publication made possible
with the assistance of the Kern Foundation*

THE THEOSOPHICAL PUBLISHING HOUSE
Wheaton, Ill., U. S. A.
Madras, India / London, England

First Quest Edition published by the Theosophical Publishing House, Wheaton, Illinois, a department of The Theosophical Society in America, 1977.

Library of Congress Cataloging in Publication Data

Chaudhuri, Haridas.
  The evolution of integral consciousness.

  (A Quest book)
  Bibliography: p.
  Includes index.
  1. Consciousness. I. Title.
BF311.C513   126   77-4219
ISBN 0-8356-0494-2

Printed in the United States of America

This book is dedicated to
Bina Chaudhuri
whose strength, compassion, and support
help to make visions into realities.

TABLE OF CONTENTS

FOREWORD by John W. White.................9

INTRODUCTION 13

PHILOSOPHY

A. The Role of Philosophy 15
B. The Integral Theory of Being 23
C. The Integral View of Consciousness 33

HISTORY

A. The Meaning of History 43
B. The Law of Cosmic Balance 49

PSYCHOLOGY

A. Integral Psychology 59
B. Individuality—Relatedness—Transcendence 73

EDUCATION

A. Education of the Whole Man 77
B. International Community Education 83

METHODOLOGY

A. The Integral Method 85
B. Integral Dialectics 92

SCIENCE

A. Quantum Theory and Consciousness 103
B. Brain Research and Integration of
       Consciousness 112
C. The Scientific Method 115

ONTOLOGICAL DISCIPLINE

A. Being-Realization 117
B. Meditation for Integral Self-Development 121

EPILOGUE

A. The Future of Civilization 131
B. Notes on the Influence of Sri Aurobindo 135

REFERENCES AND NOTES.....................137

FOREWORD

For someone seriously engaged in the exploration of consciousness, contact with Dr. Haridas Chaudhuri is inevitable. That is because he stands on the mountaintop among a small group of modern consciousness explorers whose lifelong efforts have brought them into an exalted state of supreme knowledge and effortless, integrated practice of that knowledge.

I was fortunate to meet Dr. Chaudhuri in person. After communicating via mail for a year, I met him and his wife, Bina, in 1973. In company with psychologist Dr. Allan Cohen, we enjoyed an evening of stimulating conversation. Our talk ranged over many of the topics which are presented here at greater length. That meeting and the too-few others I had with Dr. Chaudhuri produced many warm memories. I am truly grateful for this opportunity to recommend the work of my friend and teacher to a wider audience.

Although I describe him as my teacher, I was never formally a student of Dr. Chaudhuri. Nevertheless, our relations showed me that he was not only a scholar and academic of the finest sort, but also that he possessed many of the qualities that humanity at large has traditionally admired as indicative of a self-realized person. It was deeply gratifying to be in his presence. One learned from his very being, as well as his keen intellect, and learning had to do with the most fundamental aspect of existence—consciousness.

Since this book is entitled *The Evolution of Integral Consciousness*, you might ask, "What is consciousness—this element that is to be expanded and integrated?" Dr. Chaudhuri provided a clear answer. "Consciousness," he once said, "is the essential structure of the human psyche. It is something which is the common denominator of all the levels of the human psychic structure. Consciousness is the essential structure of human reality. And all that we do outside of us in our human relations, social activities, or building up social, political and international structures, is ultimately determined by the dynamics of the human psyche. So this is the point of view from which we have to approach the whole subject."

This statement explains clearly why it is important to explore consciousness. In order to know reality, you must examine the means whereby you know: consciousness. For those who choose to, it can be extremely valuable to have a map or set of guidelines with which to orient yourself. *The Evolution of Integral Consciousness* provides just that—a precise and reliable instrument with which to find your way through the dense underbrush of conflicting ideologies and dogmas that have sprung up profusely of late.

Another statement by Dr. Chaudhuri is appropriate for closing this Foreword. "In the course of the development of the human being, there comes a time when the question 'Who am I?' comes to the forefront of his mind. 'What is the essence of my being? What is my potential and the purpose of life? What is my position in society or in the total scheme of existence?' These are questions vital to the consciousness of man."

Reason, research and personal experience have convinced me that Dr. Chaudhuri is quite correct in his analysis. More important, he has gone beyond analysis to synthesis. He has answers as well as questions—answers that ring true all the way to rock-bottom reality—and he provides them here for the inquiring reader in a loving, nondogmatic way. I therefore now invite you to get on with your exploration of consciousness, knowing that you are being guided by a wise and noble man.

John White

ACKNOWLEDGMENTS

This volume has been a project of people interested in the area of Integral and Interdisciplinary Studies at the California Institute of Asian Studies in San Francisco. Assistance in typing, transcriptions, and editing has been helpfully rendered by Virgina Barnes, Judy Rozhon, Tom Volenik, Jim Sierra, Walt Eels, Dhruva Watson, Shipra Chaudhuri, and Mrs. Bina Chaudhuri.

We are grateful to the Board of Governors of the Cultural Integration Fellowship for allowing use of the material gathered from lectures by Dr. Chaudhuri given under their auspices. We are also grateful to the *Community Education Journal* for an extract from the article "International Community Education", appearing in their July-August 1975 issue, and to the *International Philosophical Quarterly* for their permission to incorporate "The Integral View of Consciousness", which was first published in the June 1970 issue.

The Editors

INTRODUCTION

The Evolution of Integral Consciousness is a collection of articles, mostly unpublished, and transcripts of talks given by the late Dr. Haridas Chaudhuri at the California Institute of Asian Studies and the Cultural Integration Fellowship in San Francisco, both of which he founded and directed until his passing in the spring of 1975.

A philosopher, humanist and educator of true evolutionary vision, Dr. Chaudhuri's life was dedicated to synthesis and integration on all levels—from personal psychodynamics through the various fields of knowledge to cultural unity. Although there has always been a gratifying amount of interest in his works, since his death there has been an increased awareness of the potency of his perspective and its relevance for our society. That perspective is succinctly stated in his own words:

> We are witnessing today a widespread spiritual awakening, not only in this country, but in other parts of the world. This widespread search is a very significant thing. It implies that we have come to a point in evolution and history where there is the possibility of the emergence of a new light of consciousness. Just as one day a human being endowed with rational self-consciousness evolved out of the matrix of animal consciousness, and built his society, culture and civilization, so, too, we have now come to a point of evolution when there are signs and indications that a still-higher level and power of consciousness is likely to be manifested, laying the foundation of a new global society.

In working with this emerging image, which is both integral and evolutionary, Dr. Chaudhuri was pragmatically concerned with the growth of human awareness and of the potentials that are latent in the human being. He focused on drawing from his students and associates a personal, conscious participation in the creative expression of their capacities. The need for an expansion and integration of consciousness was seen by him as an unavoidable necessity for resolving the conflicts we are presently facing.

The integral perspective is also concerned with encouraging harmony among people by showing that there is room for a multiplicity of perspectives and styles of life within an encompassing human unity. Dr. Chaudhuri's goal of bridging the gap between East and West brought him to the United States in 1951, and throughout the years he continued to implement his ever-finer perceptions of the nature of successful intercultural understanding. Further, the view represented here attempts to link divergent systems of thought through appreciating their varying methods as well as in recognizing an underlying common foundation of principles. With this in mind, he has brought out recent discoveries in scientific thinking in ways which may be easily assimilated into our conscious awareness. As he once said, "Truth is eternal—but with the changing intellectual and cultural climates in different countries, there is the need for developing different conceptual frameworks suitable to the changing conditions of history. To express and articulate effectively the eternal truth—this is part of the Integral Method."

Dr. Chaudhuri was one of those rare human beings who manifested the integral consciousness of which he spoke and wrote. He was seen by those around him as a profoundly sensitive scholar and most illumined individual. At a time when positive and guiding images of the future are vital to the welfare of humanity, his contributions in that regard make this book a unique and valuable contribution.

Dionne Marx and
Dave Kendall

PHILOSOPHY

If you believe that man is a child of nature, a product of terrestrial evolution, then it will be very reasonable to assume that the deepest aspirations of the human soul have some organic relationship to nature. Those aspirations which persist are probably a reflection in human consciousness of the potentials of evolution. These dreams of our minds show which way the process of evolution is going.

A. THE ROLE OF PHILOSOPHY

The value of philosophy as detached contemplation of the totality of existence has been seriously called into question in modern times. The immensely accelerated tempo of living inclines one to look upon philosophic contemplation as an idle intellectual pastime. Caught up in the breathtaking speed of fast moving international events, people have little patience today for sustained concentration and silent communion with the timeless. The mounting pressure of the problems of the jet age combined with the enchantment of ever-newer gadgets and push-button comforts seems to have rendered philosophic meditation outmoded and old-fashioned.

Certain vociferous tendencies in contemporary thinking seem to take great pleasure in pointing the finger of scorn to metaphysical reflections. Some maintain that metaphysics as a *weltanschauung* or comprehensive world-view is nothing but "sublimated mythology." Some hold that philosophy as the interpretation of the nature of existence is a colossal waste of human energy, because what we need first and foremost is action and desirable change of our environment through appropriate action. Some hold that philosophy conceived as the metaphysics of God, Absolute, Self, etc., is not only a false pursuit but just meaningless verbiage or nonsensical jargon insofar as these notions are incapable of verification in terms of concrete experience. Metaphysical concepts are worse than false inasmuch as they are beyond the range of sense experience.

In keeping with the same line of thinking, value judgements involving truth, beauty, goodness, holiness, etc., are often branded as mere "emotional ejaculations" void of any objective experiential content. When one says "God is good," or "Truth is one," or "The flower is beautiful," and the like, such statements express only our subjective feelings and afford no insight into the structure of reality. Thus we see philosophy has fallen upon very evil days indeed! Perhaps no worse crisis is conceivable for the spirit of philosophic inquiry.

May it be that this abysmal misfortune of philosophy is precisely at the root of the crisis of our present age? May it be that it is this contemptuous rejection of philosophy in the mad pursuit of technological exploits and mass organization which has created today the worst crisis in history? Ours seems to be the age of ever-increasing anxiety and fear. It is an age of rising standards of living and vanishing awareness of the purpose of life.

If the crux of our present-day crisis lies in the loss of higher values, and if the essential function of philosophy is to inquire into the meaning of life in the total scheme of existence, philosophy can certainly play an important role. The classical role of the philosopher in every historical epoch has been to reconstruct higher values on the basis of a clear understanding of the crucial problems of that epoch, to reaffirm the truth in a language intelligible to contemporary society and in a form appropriate to the intellectual and social climate of the day.

Philosophy as Integration of Knowledge

Philosophy can help modern man in maintaining his sense of proportion and in developing a balanced perspective in respect of recent developments in the various specialized fields of knowledge. Every field of knowledge—and there is ever-increasing specialization and subdivision of knowledge today—has its own special categories. In the absence of adequate training in philosophic thinking, a person devoted to a special field of investigation has an unconscious tendency to invest with ultimate significance the category appropriate to his own field. And thus he falls into the trap of dogmatism and intolerant parochialism. For instance, a physicist has the tendency to apply the category of matter or physical energy to the understanding of all life and the totality of Being. A biologist has the tendency to apply the category of life or élan vital to the understanding of the totality of existence. A psychologist has the tendency to apply the category of mind or consciousness to the interpretation of the whole of reality. A logician is too often inclined to exalt to the highest rank the category of idea or reason and make it the essence of reality.

Similarly, whereas ethics is prone to emphasize the sovereign reality of the concept of goodness, religion uses the notion of the divine or the holy as a key to the inmost structure of the universe. In stressing the reality of higher values, both ethics and religion are prone to ignore the fundamental oneness of existence and the unbroken continuity of the cosmic process. In affirming the primacy of spiritual value, they are inclined to turn a blind eye to the spirit of nature and her secret wisdom.

Philosophy as criticism of categories can prevent our human knowledge from degenerating into parochial absolutism. It endeavors to coordinate and harmonize the divergent standpoints of science, psychology, logic, ethics, religion, etc. It shows how different categories appropriate to different branches of knowledge reveal different aspects of the same multi-form existence. It points out that ultimate reality is not to be identified with either matter or life or mind or reason or value. At the same time, these categories are not to be dismissed as just subjective constructions or mere modes of human apprehension. They certainly afford insights into the multi-dimensional richness of Being.

An adequate comprehension of reality in its multi-form and multi-dimensional fullness can alone lay the foundation for an integrated scheme of human values. In trying to develop such a comprehensive vision of truth, philosophy can serve as a powerful deterrent to the present-day fragmentation of life and the increasing subdivision of knowledge.

Philosophy is essentially a thinking about human thinking. It is called upon to pass in review, with a view to critical evaluation, diversified ideas and thought-systems. The value of such a critical survey is that it preserves what is essential in man's heritage and at the same time indicates future lines of development and further progress. It recognizes the imperishable elements of truth revealed in different thought-systems of the past. At the same time, it rises above the past by understanding that all thought-systems are only inadequate and imperfect expressions of the total truth.

Reality is essentially beyond all verbalized expression or logical articulation. It is *nirguna* (i.e., indeterminable and non-verbal), as Vedanta puts it. It is, to use a very suggestive term of Karl Jaspers, the Comprehensive,[1] and as such beyond the subject-object differentiation. All thought-systems as verbalized structures are objects of reflective consciousness, and, for that very reason, none of them can be exhaustively expressive of the fullness of Being. Having risen above the past and making a fresh contact with the unfathomable, philosophy prepares the ground for new spiritual progress and opens new horizons in the realm of the spirit.

The truth with which philosophy deals is eternally old and yet perpetually new. In every age the timeless truth has to be couched in words appropriate to the emergent evolutionary condition of that age. In every country it has to be articulated in a form that would particularly suit the specific social and intellectual conditions of that country. With the passing of time, and the consequent changing of the human situation, a particular formulation of philosophical truth may grow somewhat out of date. It gets petrified in a fixed form and objective structure. And thus arises the need for a fresh contact with the formless truth which is pure transcendence. The essential function of the philosopher is to deliver a new message out of the depths of eternity—a message which would indicate the main lines of future development on the foundation provided by the past; a message which would reaffirm the timeless truth in the appropriate mold of the present times.

Philosophy as the Basis of Human Unity

Philosophy can help man in developing a cosmic perspective toward the building of a global unity. Philosophy can create that intellectual climate under which people can learn more and more to live as citizens of the same world, or as members of one human family. The philosopher can nourish this goal by making people aware of their essential inter-relatedness, thereby releasing vast unifying potentials.

Religion, with its concepts of the fatherhood of God and the brotherhood of man or with its emphasis upon the oneness of all existence and the spirit of universal love, contains within itself the dynamics of human unity. Divorced from the critical self-understanding of philosophic reflection, religion has a tendency to degenerate into sectarianism, dogmatism, fanaticism, aggressive proselytization, and the like. A religious leader so often seems to think that the unification of the human race can only be brought about under the aegis of his own particular religious faith. Instead of contributing to human unity, such narrow and dogmatic religious ideas erect walls of division between man and man, generate mutual hatred and hostility, and encourage bigotry. It is dismaying to note that even today there are fanatical evangelists who fly around the world preaching in dead earnest that the hope of salvation for the whole of mankind lies in accepting their particular brand of religious creed.

It is worth observing here that in India, religion has always moved hand in hand with philosophy. In consequence, out of the profoundest religious and mystical experiences India has developed an all-comprehensive spiritual outlook which emphasizes the essential harmony of all religions and affirms the one indivisible Truth which is the common substratum of different faiths.

It is this message of philosophical religion, if I may use such as expression, which has to be more and more understood all over the world today. It implies that the apparently divergent conceptions of God elaborated in the theological systems of the different religions are but different modes of intellectual formulation of the same fundamental spiritual reality of the universe which is the source of all higher values. It implies that the essentials of religion consist in affirming the spiritual oneness of all existence, the rootedness of all individuals and races in the identity of one universal spirit, and the supremacy of such values as truth, love, peace, harmony, freedom, justice, etc.

Philosophical religion further maintains that God is not to be exclusively identified with any particular historical figure such as Buddha, Krishna, Christ, Moses, Mohammed, etc.

They are all manifestations in history of the one supra-historical creative intelligence that guides the course of history. Also, it is sheer human ignorance to debate about the superiority of this or that particular prophet or avatar. All avatars are equal insofar as all of them are manifestations of the same world-spirit in different historical epochs, each fulfilling his specific role with eminent success on the historical stage. The achievements of the different avatars are not to be compared one with another without reference to their special historical settings.

Similarly, no sacred scripture of any particular religion can be regarded as an exhaustive revelation of the absolute truth. Each religious scripture is intended to provide spiritual nourishment to growing souls and earnest truth seekers. As an individual attains maturity of spiritual understanding, he goes beyond the confines of the written or spoken word and discovers the non-verbal truth in the silent depths of his inner consciousness. As Martin Heidegger has put it, he begins to hear "the soundless voice of Being".[2] This non-verbal truth, the creative logos, the "soundless voice of Being", is what Tantra has called *Anahata*, the uncreated and supra-causal wisdom. It is human stupidity to think of truth as the monopoly of any particular individual, or group, or race, or organization.

Truth is the spiritual potentiality and divine heritage of all mankind. The function of each religious faith is to help men to realize this divine heritage of man. In adequately performing this function, religion fulfills itself beyond itself. The spiritually integrated individual advances from the particularity of religious faith in which he was born to the universality of spiritual outlook as the full flowering of his faith.

Philosophy and World Peace

In modern times, religious faith has yielded to a far more powerful force in collective living, and that is political ideology. Political ideology means in our present age what religious creed meant in medieval times. It is the most dynamic factor today in the sphere of social action and international relations. Consequently, the most crucial problem facing humanity in our present age is the problem in interrelationship between such rival ideologies as communism and democracy, or socialism and capitalism. With the creation of hydrogen bombs and rockets, the problem has assumed alarming proportions so that it poses a menace not only to the peace of the world, but to the very survival of the human race.

Philosophy can advance the cause of world peace by critically examining and eliminating the unconscious roots of the war mentality. One devious root of war-mindedness is the dualistic logic of the arrogant intellect—the logic of either/or. Dualistic logic says: Either communism or democracy, either socialism or capitalism, is the ultimate truth, and thus creates an irreconcilable opposition between them, dividing the world into two warring camps sworn to destroy each other. At the prompting of the logic of either/or, even well-meaning humanitarians and philanthropists are sometimes out to convert the world to their own ideology and feel justified to liquidate the members of the opposite camp, considered as implacable enemies of humanity.

Under the influence of dualistic logic, one comes to believe that if a group or nation does not accept capitalistic democracy it must be sold on communism; and likewise, if it does not embrace communism it must be a lackey of capitalism. Similarly, if a group or nation is a friend of the USA it must be an enemy of the USSR, and on the contrary, if it be a friend of the USSR it must be an enemy of the USA. A philosophic understanding of the nature of truth and existence can produce what may be called the outlook of nondualism.

Nondualism implies that seemingly conflicting political ideologies are only relatively valid truths of life. None of them can be affirmed to represent the absolute truth. On the other hand, none of them can be condemned either as absolute untruth. Each represents a particular formulation of truth based upon the consideration of some specific social, economical and political conditions useful in a particular country at a given time. There may be a host of other ideologies existing in between them and answering to the divergent needs and problems of other countries. Such other ideologies would suitably incorporate into themselves the elements of truth and value to be found in both communism and democracy, giving rise to the concepts of mixed economy, socialistic democracy, etc.

Philosophical understanding would reveal how an endless

variety of ideologies can be reconciled in the nondualistic structure of life, in accordance with the specific needs and survival problems of different life forms. Dualistic logic is based upon the fallacy of identification of idea with reality, whereas nondualistic philosophy reveals the essence of reality as beyond the realm of ideas. Dualistic logic generates an exclusive, aggressive, and militant attitude, whereas nondualism produces an all-embracing, all-reconciling, peace-loving attitude of the mind. Inherent in nondualism is the power of reconciliation of a multiplicity of ideologies and thought systems which are valid relative to the varying conditions of empirical existence.

Another root cause of the war mentality is the fear complex which haunts the powerful nations of the world today. That is why well-meaning politicians may sincerely talk about peace, and yet feverishly prepare for war. They are just suspicious and afraid of one another. The greater the fear, the greater the sharpening of weapons, and the sharper the weapons, the greater the fear. What is the way out of this ever-widening vicious circle?

According to spiritual philosophy, the only way out of this vicious circle is increasing reliance upon the principle of non-violence, *ahimsa*, as the sovereign means of solving all international disputes. Every time a leading politician emphasizes the value of honest and peaceful negotiation above the practice of political double-dealing and sabre-rattling, a precious stone is laid in the foundation of world peace. Hatred breeds hatred, violence begets violence, an atmosphere of mutual suspicion and fear stimulates the darkest subterranean forces of human nature. On the contrary, active faith in the power of truth and love can release miraculous powers of transformation in the direction of fruitful cooperation. The principle of nonviolence is the practical application of the philosophical concept of nondualism.

Philosophy can serve the cause of peace and progress by providing man with a balanced system of values. When people are too much wedded to the material values of existence, ignoring the higher spiritual values of life, they are always ready to fight with each other with all the destructive weapons at their disposal. Unmitigated materialism launches men on the path of mutual destruction. When on the other hand people are too much enamored of the transcendent spiritual values—ignoring the reality and significance of the material, social, economical and political aspects of life—society is more and more left in the hands of power hungry and self-seeking individuals. This creates a split society with philosophers and sages withdrawn and indifferent, and with kings and rulers scheming for power and domination. Negative spiritualism strikes at the roots of social, economical, and political progress.

By properly and adequately integrating the values of time and eternity, philosophy can render the spiritual forces of the world more and more effective in shaping the affairs of mankind. An integrated scheme of values is certainly of paramount importance in transforming human society into an abode of peace and love and freedom continously productive of higher values.

B. *THE INTEGRAL THEORY OF BEING*

The concept of Being can be viewed from the perspectives of the temporal and nontemporal or from time and eternity. From the temporal perspective, Being appears as an evolutionary hierarchy of increasingly marvelous spheres of existence such as the material, the vital, the mental, the rational, and the spiritual. Samuel Alexander in his *Space, Time, and Deity*[3] presents an evolutionary theory of Being. In recent times Pierre Teilhard de Chardin has done the same.[4] These views may be described as the temporal-evolutionary theory of Being.

However, an analysis of the structure of time may also lead to a profound ontological understanding of Being as we find in Martin Heidegger's *Being and Time*. He perceives time as "the transcendental horizon for the problem of Being".[5] He experiences Being as the ground of all things and beings enduring in time. His view may be described as the temporal-ontological theory of Being.

From the nontemporal perspective, the Vedantic-Buddhist tradition of India encounters Being through some such transtemporal experience as samadhi or bodhi (enlightenment). The result is the doctrine of Being as the ultimate ground of the universe beyond space, time and causation. This view may be described as the nontemporal-ontological theory of Being.

The integral view of Being, briefly outlined here, is a reconciliation of the temporal and nontemporal perspectives. In this outlook Being is multidimensional. The nontemporal ground of existence and the evolutionary movement of time are equally real dimensions of Being. The views mentioned above are really dealing with different aspects of the same multi-faceted Being.

Let us first elucidate the meaning of the word Being. Being is indeed the most fundamental category of thought, yet most bewildering is the variety of its meanings.

Hegel starts his philosophical speculation dialectically with the concept of Being. He uses the notion of being as the summon genus[6] under which everything that is can be classified. It is the common denominator of everything that is. In this sense it has the widest and most comprehensive denotation but at the same time the poorest content or connotation. Being which is nothing in particular but everything in general—Being which is void of all determinations—is indeed indistinguishable from non-being or nothing. Upon close reflection being passes into nothing or non-being. But non-being again, insofar as it is an object of thought, discloses itself as being.[7]

The word Being may also be used to denote determinate structures of existence. Different species of animals and races of men are beings. Atoms and molecules, cells and societies are beings. Oceans and mountains, suns and planets, stars and galaxies are also beings.

Then again the word Being may include in its signification not only actual existents but also ideal subsistents. Actual existing things like rivers and mountains, trees and animals, are what they are because they occupy definite positions in the space-time continuum. As occupants of space-time they are capable of being perceived. Now as opposed to such actual existents there are subsistent entities like laws and principles, platonic essences and ideas, concepts and truths of mathematical sciences, and the like. Even dream objects and imaginary things which abound in poetry, art, and works of fiction subsist in the sense of being objective termini of our mental acts of imagination. They are certainly not just mental processes or modifications. They have some kind of ideal or conceptual being.

The word Being with a capital *B* is often used to mean God, the Supreme Being. However, the Supreme Being conceived as the owner of such divine qualities as wisdom, love perfection, justice, etc., is also a determinate mode of being. He is a being, not Being as such. The Supreme Being or God conceived as one infinite and permanent spiritual substance endowed with numerous divine qualities and as the first cause of the world is evidently an intellectual construction, a theory, a conceptual interpretation of religious experience. It is the result of our application of the categories of substance and cause to ultimate reality.

Finally, Being is used in the ontological sense to signify not a being, but Being as such. Being is the ultimate ground of all beings. It is not the "beingness" of beings. It is not the summon genus which is the thinest of all abstractions. Nor is it the sum total of all beings, because the sum total or aggregation of beings is an abstract arithmetical notion and not the concrete sustaining medium of beings. Nor is it God who has a determinate mode of being. Being is the ground of all beings without itself being a being, just as the space-time continuum is the ground of all things without itself being a thing.

Being, as Martin Heidegger points out, is not identical with beings or the beingness of beings, nor is it opposed to them. Being is not the way things are, but that which makes whatever is real to be real.[8] This Heideggerian concept of Being is closely similar to the Upanisadic concept of Brahman or Being (*Tat Sat*) as the ultimate ground of all that is. It is that from which all beings are born, that by which when born they live, and that which when departing, they enter.[9] It is in this sense that the word Being is used here.

Being is reality in its multidimensional fullness. Broadly speaking there are two dimensions of Being. First, Being is revealed as time, as cosmic energy, as the evolutionary process. Secondly, Being is revealed as the timeless ground of the cosmic manifold, as the indeterminable silence or void.

Cosmic energy reveals the glory of Being in various forms as divergent spheres of existence. Cosmic energy is Being in its primordial manifestation. In Sanskrit language this is called *Prakriti* or *Shakti*. Cosmic energy in its essential structure is neither physical nor spiritual. It is neutral to such distinctions and dichotomies. Both matter and mind, body and soul, the physical and the psychical, emerge in the course of evolution out of cosmic energy.

Is this cosmic energy blind? It is neither blind nor reflectively conscious like man. There is a principle of immanent finality operative in cosmic energy. It is due to this principle of immanent finality or unconscious wisdom embedded in cosmic creative energy that flowers blossom, that life emerges out of physical and chemical forces, and that consciousness breaks forth with its unique effulgence out of the cerebral processes of the nervous system.

Is this immanent finality the somnambulistic action of the spirit fallen asleep in nature? Is it the wisdom of God secretly operative in matter? Or is it an illusion created by the casting and re-casting of the cosmic weather, a false impression generated by the fortuitous combinations and recombinations of blind mechanical forces jostling with one another? Who can tell?

Is cosmic energy rational or irrational? Perhaps both. The distinction between rational and irrational is valid only as relative to the human mind. The human mind has a certain mode of operation which follows laws of consistency such as the Aristotelian laws of logic. Whatever is subservient to the cherished goals of human life such as personal or species survival, pursuit of happiness and liberty, etc., is good. Those cosmic events which are in keeping with these laws of logic and goals of life appear rational to us. The contrary events we call irrational. For instance the luxuriant growth of crops in the life-and-warmth-giving sunshine and nourishing showers is rational and good. On the other hand, floods and earthquakes, droughts and famines, are irrational and evil. The truth of the matter is that in the structure of cosmic energy both rational and irrational forces, powers of light and darkness, intermingle. Gods and demons dwell there side by side.

Cosmic energy is indeed an enormously complex unity of radically opposite forces. There is the unitive impulse as well as the disintegrating force. The unitive impulse makes electrons and protons combine into atoms; atoms combine into molecules; divergent molecules combine into living cells;

multitudinous cells combine into self-regulating organisms. The unitive impulse is the impulse of life and love.

Besides the unitive impulse, there is also the divisive, disintegrating force. It pulls down all differentiated structures back into the simplicity of undifferentiated homogeneity. It is the force of death and destruction. So, the cosmic process becomes the dynamic interplay of life and death, of union and dissolution.

These radically opposite forces of attraction and repulsion are constantly operative in nature. The force of attraction holds together planets and satellites in the solar system; it holds together different solar systems and stars in the galaxies. But along side of the force of attraction, there is also a tremendous force of repulsion active on the cosmic scene. By virtue of this force of repulsion different galaxies are tearing away from each other with enormous speed. It is this intergalactic running away which makes our universe a constantly expanding one.

Cosmic energy is the essential structure of nature. It is Being in its primordial expression. Some philosophers are inclined to equate Being with cosmic energy or nature. This gives rise to naturalism or energism. Our contention is that a fallacy is committed here—the fallacy of false equation. Energy or nature is a particular mode of manifestation, a specific dimension of Being. But it is a manifest error to equate it with Being.

Nature in its simplest expression is a perpetual dance of energy. It is constant mobility and change, flux and flow. As the elements of energy, like atoms and molecules, combine in stable structures with fixed forms and visible marks of distinction, material substances come into existence. We may say that material substances are specific configurations of energy endowed with the emergent quality of materiality.

Some philosophers are inclined to equate Being with material substance. In their view, matter is ultimate reality. "Everything comes out of matter, everything abides in matter, and everything is dissolved in matter again",[10] as Bhrigu says on the dawning of his first metaphysical insight in the Taittiriya Upanishad. "Matter contains the promise and potency of all terrestrial life"[11] as Tyndall says.

Now the material world within multitudinous stable material structures such as mountains and valleys, stars and galaxies, is indeed a definite form of manifestation—the material dimension of Being. To equate Being with matter, however, is also a false equation. Being is indeed matter, but it is also beyond matter. It exists before matter and also surpasses matter by its own boundless creativity.

In the course of evolution, new qualities and values emerge. As the material forces combine and re-combine reaching a higher degree of complexity of structure and function, the novel quality of vitality manifests itself. Enormously complex material structures endowed with vitality give rise to the world of living things such as plants and trees. They grow and develop from within by assimilating elements of nourishment from without. They evince powers of self-healing and self-reproduction. This organic world is a higher grade of manifestation of Being. It is Being revealed as the universal life force, as the élan vital, as *prana*.

Some philosophers are inclined to equate Being with the universal life force. This gives rise to vitalism. The élan vital (*prana*) is that "from which everything comes into being, in which everything abides, and into which everything is dissolved again", as Bhrigu says at the second stage of his sustained quest of Being.[12] Henri Bergson, the French philosopher, has the same inclination. For him the élan vital is the ultimate reality.

But here again the comment should be made that to equate Being with the universal life force is to commit the fallacy of false equation. The organic world is without a doubt a marvelous form of manifestation of Being, but it is certainly not co-extensive with Being. Vital energy is an ontological power of Being, but not the total reality of Being.

As the forces of the organic world attain a higher degree of complexity of structure and function in the course of evolution, another novel quality emerges—the quality of sentient consciousness (*manas*). Psychical energy dominated by instincts and the senses appears as a new development and lays the foundation for the animal kingdom, including thousands of species lower and higher.

Being is now manifested as sentient consciousness or instinctual energy.[13] There are some philosophers who identify Being with instinctual psychism and develop instinctualism as the dominant outlook. The seemingly higher faculties of man such as intellect, reason, moral sense, religious consciousness and spiritual insight are explained in terms of the instinctual urges of sex, survival, power drive, aggressiveness, etc.

There are some philosophers who, having identified Being with sentient consciousness, develop some sort of empirical idealism or positivism as the dominant world-view. Sensations or sense data are believed to be the stuff of which the world is made. The whole choir of heaven and furniture of earth are explained in terms of sensations, sense data and sensible phenomena.

But a broad survey of reality is sure to bring home the truth that to equate Being with sentient experience is like trapping space in a bottle. Space is certainly enclosed in the bottle, but it also boundlessly transcends the bottle. Animal consciousness, instinctual psychic energy, the world of sense experience, etc., are certainly valid modes of manifestation of Being. But they can hardly be said to exhaust the multiform fullness of Being.

As the forces of instinctual energy attain through the course of further evolution to a still higher degree of complexity of structure and function, another amazing development takes place. The unprecedented value and quality of reason or rational self-consciousness emerges. As an enormously complex configuration of psychic energy, man appears on the cosmic scene, endowed with this new power—reason.

Being is now manifested as universal reason or logos. As a result, a new order of creation, a new pattern of existence springs up. An unforeseen new world—the world of man and his creative imagination, with his history of culture and civilization—emerges. Universal reason is objectivized as the realm of eternal ideas and essences, or as the absolute idea embracing in an inclusive synthesis all the structural principles of existence as conceived by reason. It illuminates reality as the realm of logical principles and scientific laws, ethical standards and religious creeds, social utopias and political ideologies.

On this level, reason is the sovereign ruler. Ideas as the offspring of reason ultimately determine the behavioral patterns of men as thinking beings. However, reason is riddled with self-contradictions. Consequently ideas can hardly achieve the goals that reason projects.

Reason is self-contradictory. It claims to fathom the mystery of Being by thinking. But thinking always presupposes the concrete facts of experience, whether sensuous or super-sensuous, whether perceptual or transcendental. These concrete facts of experience are just immediately given. They are non-rational data, incapable of being derived from reason. Obviously then these data of sense experience and the total of transcendental awareness fall outside rational thinking.

Even though the ideas of reason aim to unify life and reality, they often meet with failure. From the dawn of civilization, different religions have been trying to unify mankind with their different ideas of God. But instead of establishing a universal brotherhood, they often divide humanity into mutually exclusive and often bitterly antagonistic religious communities. Each political ideology claims to unify humanity under its own banner. But in actual practice we find a series of violently clashing political ideologies creating a war-hysteria in the name of world peace. This is bound to be so because ideas and ideologies, which can never bridge the gulf between thought and reality, can hardly infuse into life and evolution the authentic spirit of totality and comprehensive unity.

There are other indications why reason, by itself, can hardly fulfill man's age-long aspiration for the kingdom of heaven on earth, that is, for a unique world order of peace, justice, and international harmony. Inherent in the human psyche there are irrational impulses including the death instinct as Freud has discovered. That is why while professing love we practice hatred. While striving for peace we make preparations for war; when in an atmosphere of peace and happiness we feel suffocated and experience an irrational urge to destroy our own heaven.

Man gets quickly disillusioned about the efficacy of thought or reason as the ruling principle of life. At an enormous cost of personal and historical suffering, he becomes aware of its limitations. He looks beyond logic to the higher reaches of Being. He reaches out for deeper penetration into the mystery of life and evolution. The truth increasingly dawns upon him that for man to be fully human, for him to establish an international human family wedded to the ideals of freedom, justice, peace and progress, there has to be a radical change of inner consciousness illuminated by the creative light of Being itself.

This brings us to the possibility of a spiritual mutation in the human species—the possibility of a major breakthrough in human evolution. Reason has no doubt performed an important function in the evolutionary process, bringing into play the infinite variety of human nature, and endless possibilities of human development. It has helped individuals to become aware of their unique and distinctive features. It has inspired the formation of different groups and communities, religious, cultural, and political organizations crystallized around different ideals of self-perfection and social progress. It has also projected the ideals of total human unity and interracial, interreligious, and international harmony. But a power of consciousness higher than reason, a power of consciousness capable of embracing all differences in a comprehensive and creative unity, is essentially needed to fulfill reason's ideal of inclusive unity in diversity.

In the Taittiriya Upanishad[14] we find that Bhrigu in his sustained quest of Being, finally advances beyond reason or the realm of ideals and laws. He transcends the furthest boundaries of the rational mind and attains to transcendental awareness of Being in its essential structure. Such transcendental awareness is known as spiritual enlightenment, turiya, bodhi, satori, etc. In transcendental awareness of Being, the dichotomy of subject and object is finally transcended. One knows Being by becoming one with it or by realizing that the knower, in his inmost essence, is no different from Being.

Having thus known Being by becoming one with it, one becomes speechless. This is because one realizes that all the normal categories of thought such as substance and attribute, cause and effect, one and many, etc. are inapplicable here. One also realizes that the categories of religious consciousness such as God and soul, spirit and permanence, personality and love, are inapplicable here. Being just *is*. And yet Being is inseparable from Becoming.

To authentic transcendental awareness, Being is revealed as Ananda—that is, infinite joy, the boundless ocean of bliss.

"Everything arises from the fullness of joy in the heart of reality, everything abides in joy, and everything is dissolved and fulfilled in joy again,"[15] says Bhrigu, the great adventurer in the realm of truth. There is no subject-object distinction in the ocean of Being. It is nondual awareness of the ultimate ground of the universe, discovering the ultimate meaning of life and the supreme value of existence. It is the kind of bliss which has both a static and a dynamic aspect.

Awareness of Being in its nontemporal dimension produces the bliss of immutable being, of suchness, the bliss of perfect serenity. Whereas, the awareness of Being in its aspect of Becoming, as dynamic self-expression in time, engenders bliss in the form of creative joy, the joy of manifesting the eternal in time. It is the bliss of ecstatic and transpersonal experience of pure transcendence.

History bears testimony to many sages and mystics the world over hailing from different religions and different countries, having attained glimpses of Being as the ultimate ground of all existence. Such glimpses have transformed their personal lives and released great forces of love and truth. But masses of humanity have continued more or less on the beaten track determined in their behavior patterns by fixed habits of thought.

The creative joy of Being-awareness, which contains within itself the power of embracing all differences in the creative unity of Being, has not yet become a dynamic ingredient of the collective consciousness of mankind. This has not yet become a creative force in human evolution. However, it is certainly possible that human evolution is moving precisely in that direction. Since it is the creative energy of Being itself operative in nature and history which ultimately determines the process of evolution, the probability looms large that in the foreseeable future the next leap in human evolution would consist in the overt operation of the creative light and joy of Being in guiding the affairs of mankind.

Let us now briefly sum up. Being is the ultimate ground and the comprehensive unity of all existence. Fundamentally it has two equally real and inseparable dimensions; the nontemporal and the temporal. In its nontemporal dimension Being is absolutely indeterminable, ineffable Silence, beyond all forms and images, concepts and categories. In its temporal dimension it is the cosmic process, characterized by perpetual making and breaking, creation and destruction, attraction and repulsion. On our home planet earth we observe cosmic energy assume the form of an evolutionary movement. Whereas matter forms out of energy, life evolves out of matter, mind evolves out of life, reason evolves out of mind. These represent the actualization of different dynamic potentialities of Being.

It is probable that the next breakthrough in evolution will consist in the manifestation in time of the creative self-light of Being, the integral truth-consciousness. The integrated human consciousness will be the substratum and bearer of this new ontological power of Being. It will lay the foundation for a new order of creation, a unified world-order of truth and love and justice.

C. THE INTEGRAL VIEW OF CONSCIOUSNESS

The purpose of this paper is to establish consciousness as a multi-functional emergent characteristic of the human organism. Consciousness is not a separate metaphysical principle capable of existing independently of the body or in a disembodied condition. Nor is it a mere epiphenomenon accompanying cerebral processes like a shadow, without any originality, spontaneity, and free dynamism of its own. The word 'consciousness' will be used here in its specifically human sense. It implies the kind of consciousness with which we are familiar in our human life as the common denominator of such various kinds of human experience as perception, imagination, memory, reasoning, dream, dreamless sleep, ontological awareness, mystic intuition, etc. Understood thus, consciousness is indeed a unique human category.

Consciousness as a category of human experience cannot be said to be coextensive with the entire universe. Those who believe that consciousness is coextensive with the universe use the word as an abstract metaphysical category. For instance, it is maintained by some that in atoms, molecules, minerals, plants, etc., there is a kind of implicit or involved consciousness. Teilhard de Chardin calls this the *within* of all things, the psychic face of all phenomena.[16] As in the course of evolution configurations of atoms and molecules become more and more complex and centered, their psychic temperature rises. "In the perspectives of cosmic involution, not only does consciousness become coextensive with the universe, but the universe rests in equilibrium and consistency in the form of thought on a supreme pole of interiorization."[17] Sri Aurobindo also speaks of consciousness as a universal metaphysical category. It is the essence of cosmic creative energy.

> There must be behind the action of the material energy a secret involved Consciousness, cosmic, infinite, building up through the action of that frontal Energy its means of an evolutionary manifestation, a creation out of itself in the boundless finite of the material universe.[18]

Both of these great thinkers—Chardin and Aurobindo—would agree that the type of consciousness with which we are familiar at the human level is essentially and qualitatively different from the kind of consciousness which might be present in inanimate nature or in the vegetable or animal kingdoms. Consciousness at the human level is essentially in the nature of self-luminosity. It shines by its own intrinsic light; as it reveals objects it also reveals itself as the knowing function. Man not only knows, he also knows that he knows. This lends a radically new dimension to human consciousness, making it the unique and distinctive structure of human reality.

If we adhere to the human sense of consciousness we cannot equate Being (ultimate reality) with consciousness. Being is no particular mode of existence, no determinate structure. It is the formless ground of all particular forms and modes of existence. It is the indeterminable source of all determinate structures. Consciousness as we know it is always associated with the highly developed nervous system of man. We have as yet no compelling empirical evidence demonstrating the reality of disembodied consciousness. So far as philosophic understanding goes, no body, no mind; no human brain, no consciousness. When it is said the Being is infinite or cosmic consciousness, the word consciousness is used in a Pickwickian sense. Such an equation is warranted only to prevent the misconception that Being is blind, mechanical, entirely void of all meaning and purpose.

In strictness of language all that we can say is that Being appears to us as infinite consciousness just as the sky appears to us as blue. Infinite consciousness is analogous to the blue sky. To be sure, blueness is not illusory; it is a real emergent value resulting from the interaction between the sky and the human mind. Similarly, infinite or cosmic consciousness is not an illusion; it is a real emergent value resulting from the mind's encounter with Being. The sky in its inmost structure is void of blueness. It is only capable of assuming blueness at the touch of the mind. Similarly Being in its inmost structure is absolute void or non-being (*sunyata*), as the Buddhists call it. It is absolutely formless and indeterminable (*nirguna*), as Samkara Vedanta testifies. But Being is capable of assuming the form of infinite consciousness when apprehended by the human mind.

Having thus disposed of the notion of consciousness as a specifically human category, what *is* the essential structure of consciousness? Is it always objective in orientation, or can it also shine as spontaneous luminosity without any object to shine upon? Is it essentially in the nature of detached and otiose contemplation? Or has it an intrinsic dynamism of its own by virture of which it is always out there involved in the affairs of the world, participating in the flux of life, constantly trying to change and refashion and rebuild?

Both Edmund Husserl and Jean-Paul Sartre agree that intentionality is the essential structure of consciousness.[19] Consciousness is always *consciousness of something*. The little preposition "of" implies otherness or objective orientation. Consciousness as a self-transcending function always goes beyond itself and is oriented to an Other. It is the *neosis* apprehending or intending a *noema*. I see the tree in front of my house, I fancy a trip to the moon, I dream of a lion with a man's head, I contemplate numbers in mathematical calculation. I am aware of my hunger or headache or angry mood. In all these cases some objective events or transcendent facts are intended.

A grasp of the intentional structure of consciousness liberates philosophy from solipsism or subjective idealism. It is a repudiation of the representative theory of consciousness which maintains that consciousness can directly cognize only its own modifications such as sense impressions, ideas, concepts, etc., which represent to the mind external things. Representationism when pushed to its logical extreme condemns the philosopher to the position that he and his magic circle of ideas constitute the whole of reality, the thinker being the monarch of all he surveys. Such solipsism is the philosophical version of narcissism.

Now human consciousness is also self-consciousness. Man not only knows, he also knows that he knows. In order to explain this fact, Husserl posits the notion of transcendental consciousness, and the notion of the transcendental ego as the unifying center of transcendental consciousness. But Sartre points out that it is not necessary to postulate the transcendental ego in order to explain self-awareness. Consciousness in its very act of knowing an object is also non-positionally or non-thetically aware of itself as pure subjectivity. Insofar as my reflecting consciousness is consciousness of itself, it is *non-positional* consciousness.[20] Such non-positional self-awareness is what Samuel Alexander has called "knowledge by enjoyment"[21] as distinguished from object-oriented "knowledge by contemplation". All consciousness is also self-consciousness. Objective orientation which is positional and subjective self-awareness which is non-positional are inseparable aspects of the same indivisible act of consciousness. There is no need to posit a transcendental ego in order to explain self-consciousness. Because in that case we shall need still another transcendental ego or consciousness, and then another, and so on—an infinite and endless series of them—in order to validate self-consciousness. The fallacy of infinite regress will be committed. So Sartre contends that consciousness, which simultaneously posits an object and is also aware of itself, is an absolute.

According to Sartre the ego is no part of the essential structure of consciousness. Consciousness as pure subjectivity is egoless. The ego appears on the reflected level as a synthetic complex, as an object of reflection.[22] When a person is absorbed in reading a book, in gazing at the stars, or in admiring a work of art, there is no I. When he is in anger or in love there is no I either. It is only later on when he reflects on his previous acts of reading, loving, contemplating, losing temper, etc. that the I appears as part of the complex situation such as I-was-reading, or I-was-angry, etc. Phenomenologically, all that subsequent reflection truly reveals is "there was an outburst of anger", "there was a period of absorption in reading", etc. The ego arises as an intellectual construction. It is ideally supplied to serve as the binding thread running through a flux of experiences such as reading, loving, angry behavior, etc. So Husserl, in positing a transcendental ego, departs from his original phenomenological tenet. The ego is always phenomenologically revealed to us as an object of reflection, as an ideal construction, and not as an essential part of the structure of consciousness. Consciousness as such is egoless.

Is consciousness in its essential structure the attribute of a separate mental or spiritual substance? Or is it an indefinable metaphysical principle eternally self-subsistent in character? René Descartes defines consciousness as the essential attribute of the mind as distinguished from matter. While matter is defined by extension, mind is defined in terms of consciousness. Conscious mind and extended matter are two absolutely heterogeneous substances created by God, the one infinite substance. They differ from each other by the whole diameter of their being insofar as consciousness and extension are absolutely different qualities. As a spiritual substance mind is capable of existing independently of the material body. For Descartes this prepares the ground for the personal immortality of the human individual.

Immanuel Kant points out that the conscious mind as a spiritual substance is an ideal construction of the understanding. Substance and attribute are only categories, that is to say, our human ways of interpreting the concrete facts of experience. Their scope of application is limited to the phenomenal world. It would be improper to apply them to the realm of noumena or things in themselves. Consciousness as the presupposition of all knowledge, as the prius of all interpretative acts of the understanding, is the epistemological subject. There is no logical warrant for transforming the epistemological subject into a metaphysical substance. This is a profound insight of Kant. But later on he forgets his own brilliant discovery when in deference to Christian theology he proceeds to affirm the immortality of the soul as the reality-in-itself of man. He affirms personal immortality as an article of religious faith, as the postulate of moral consciousness.

In the ancient Samkhya philosophy of India pure egoless consciousness is affirmed as the inmost self (*purusa, atman*) of the human individual. The understanding, the ego and the mind—*buddhi, ahamkara,* and *manas*—these are all regarded as the offspring resulting from the marriage between the principle of pure consciousness and unconscious nature (*prakriti*). They are evolutes of the creative dynamism of nature reflecting the light of pure consciousness. Pure consciousness is not a quality or attribute of a mental or spiritual substance. It is consciousness as such.[23] It is egoless nondiscursive consciousness. As S. Radhakrishnan says, "While the pure self remains beyond buddhi (intellect), the reflection of purusa in buddhi appears as the ego, the cognizer of all our states, pleasures and pains included".[24]

We notice here a similarity between the Samkhya view and the existentialist theory of Sartre. Both maintain the consciousness in its inmost essence is egoless. It is not a quality or attribute of any transcendent substance such as the ego or the soul. But still it is the most essential structure of human reality. It is the authentic self of the individual. Samkhya calls it *purusa*. Samkara Vendanta shares the same view and calls it *atman*. Only the latter proceeds further to equate pure consciousness (*atman*) with the supreme Being (*Brahman*).

Now as we look beneath the similarity noted above, some essential differences leap to the eye. Consciousness is indeed no-substance, no-object, no-thing. In that sense it is emptiness or nothingness. But Sartre does not indicate anywhere in his writings that consciousness which is nothingness is capable of functioning independently of the human organism or surviving the destruction of the organism. For him consciousness is strictly a phenomenological principle. But for the Samkhya and Samkara Vedanta, pure consciousness which is no-thing, no-quality, no-substance is a metaphysical principle. It is independent, self-subsistent and *causa sui*. Even though logically indefinable, it is the unmoved mover of the psychophysical dynamism of the human individual.

That brings us to the second essential point of difference. For the classical Hindu philosopher consciousness is unmoved and unmovable, unchanging and unchangeable. It is

PHILOSOPHY   39

eternally free, immortal, and self-luminous.[25] It does not require contact with external objects in order to shine as pure
consciousness. An examination of dreams discloses that consciousness functions in dreams creatively without active contact with the external world. An examination of deep dreamless sleep reveals the presence of consciousness there as the
awareness of Nothing and as the non-objective experience of
peace and bliss. That is why after a period of profound sleep a
man says, "I had a delightful, peaceful sleep", "I saw nothing
and heard nothing", and so on.

In mystic illumination or ontological experience, as inter-
preted by the classical Hindu philosophers, consciousness is
revealed as the eternally free and self-subsistent ground of
existence which shines by its own intrinsic light without any
need for external stimuli or bodily sense organs or psychic
impulses. Pure self-luminous consciousness is in this respect
like the sun. The sun does indeed shine—and shine
equally—on various objects like rivers and mountains, trees
and animals, men and supermen. But even in the absence of
all these objects, the sun would shine nonetheless. In the same
way consciousness is absolutely free and spontaneous in its
self-luminosity as well as its revelation of objects. It reveals
objects without being dependent upon them. And it can shine
even in the absence of all objects.

Like the majority of Western philosophers, Sartre has a
suspicion of mystical experience or spiritual illumination. So
he has no use for them in his philosophical construction. For a
Hindu or Buddhist philosopher, ontology as theory of Being
is inadequate without an understanding and interpretation of
the whole gamut of human experiences, including spiritual
enlightenment, which is the most dynamic and penetrative of
all experiences. Western philosophers, as a rule, have endea-
vored to develop their world-view by discounting all experiences which smack of the mystical or the supra-intellectual. So
for Sartre, consciousness is nothingness or nihilation in the
absolute sense of the term. It is a hole in being. "Consciousness continually experiences itself as the nihilation of its past
being."[26] As the contentless awareness of all objects it is the
nothing which is one with the all.[27] It cannot function apart
from, or without reference to, objects. One with the all, it is
alive only in and through absorption in the affairs of the

world. Consciousness is action. It is commitment and participation in the flux of life and social evolution. It is because
consciousness which is action is the essential structure of man
that he is constantly building and breaking and rebuilding.
He alone is capable of revolutionary changes. Always a
dreamer of new dreams he tears down the old and worn out,
sets fire to the *status quo*, envisages new possibilities and
initiates new movements.

In my view there are profound elements of truth in both the
classical Hindu view and the existentialist view. At first sight
they appear diametrically opposed. But in truth they are capable of being harmonized in a higher synthesis. Such a synthesis would be the essence of the integral view of consciousness. Consciousness in its essence is indeed egoless. It is
no-thing, no-substance, no-entity. But consciousness is
multi-functional, that is to say, capable of functioning in
different modes. It can freely adopt different attitudes and
exist in different poises. By virtue of its orientation to the
future and its vision of new possibilities, it can engage in
radical and revolutionary action. It can flow with the flux of
change and initiate radical changes by virtue of its transcendence beyond the given and the actual. But such action in
time does not exhaust the function or mode of being of consciousness.

Consciousness is also capable of taking a stand entirely
outside of the flux of change and evolution, outside of the
entire world of space-time. It can freely choose to function in a
mode of complete detachment and contemplate the nature of
existence *sub specie aeternitatis* from its stance in the void. It is
possible for consciousness to turn its attention entirely away
from the world of space, time and action and enter into communion with the timeless ground of the cosmic process.
Without an understanding of this mode of functioning of
consciousness the whole literature of original religious experience and mystic illumination, poetic intuition, and
idealistic philosophy, etc., would be reduced to meaningless
jargon.

The phenomenological view that all consciousness is objectively oriented is true of the waking consciousness of man.
But it is certainly not true of the indefinable experience of
peace that permeates dreamless sleep, which is void of all

reference to objects. It is even less true of the transcendental spiritual experience in which the light of consciousness shines by its own intrinsic light with the whole objective world put out of sight. On such a level of consciousness the world does not even appear as an illusion; it just does not appear at all. There is no reason to deny such experience as psychological fact. The error committed by world-negating mystics lies not in affirming the validity of nonobjective transcendental consciousness but in interpreting such consciousness as a separate metaphysical principle, or as the one ultimate reality, or as the total essence of Being.

It is possible that we stand today on the threshold of a new age. Old gods have died. We are passing through the twilight of transition, groping for new gods. The challenge of the times demands of man the most concerted and most illumined action. It requires the type of action which would be at once humanitarian and enlightened: humanitarian in the sense of being committed to the total welfare of mankind; enlightened in the sense of being genuinely selfless and liberated from unconscious motivations and emotional bonds. It is only a luminous awareness of Being which can bring such liberation.

The foundation of spiritual humanism is provided by what we would call the integral poise of consciousness. The transcendental poise of consciousness reveals to man the timeless essence of Being and inspires the genuinely selfless spirit of love. The existential poise of consciousness leads him to choose the line of action likely to improve the material, social, and political conditions of living in the world. The integral consciousness enables man to grasp simultaneously the timeless mystery of Being and the meaning of time. Emancipated from instinctual attachments and emotional ties, a free man is capable of taking his stand in the heart of Being. Aware of the meaning of time, he chooses the path of selfless and loving action. He actively participates in human evolution in a spirit of non-attachment. He finds himself in a position of "acting and yet not acting", "being in society and yet not of society".

Is it implied in the foregoing that pure consciousness, which is the essential structure of human reality, is an independent and immortal metaphysical principle? No. Consciousness which is capable of functioning in different modes is, as far as we know, an emergent characteristic of the human organism. It arises at the human level on the substructure of a highly developed nervous system. It is, of course, possible—but there is as yet no empirical evidence—that the human type of consciousness can exist and function independently of the human organism. When, by virtue of its transcendental poise, consciousness makes an encounter with the timeless essence of Being, it has naturally a sense of oneness with the eternal Being. Consequently it partakes of the life eternal of Being. But that does not warrant the further conclusion that the principle of consciousness can survive the death of the body and continue to live from everlasting to everlasting. The sense of immortality that a mystic possesses springs from his feeling of oneness with the eternal. Immortality is, strictly speaking, a characteristic of the eternal and not a characteristic of the consciousness which reveals the eternal. Similarly an artist or poet contemplating the timeless beauty of nature may experience a sense of immortality by virtue of his feeling of oneness with the beauty and grandeur of nature.

Whether consciousness can survive the death of its physical substructure, the body, in some other form, carried by some other configuration or subtle physical energies, is an open and debatable philosophical issue. We are knocking here at the doors of faith. Some accept on faith the doctrine of continuation of consciousness and personal immortality. They advance suitably selected arguments in its favor. Some again refuse to compromise the empirical approach. They can advance equally cogent arguments in support of the view that personal immortality is a mere illusion produced by wishful thinking.

Setting aside this debatable issue, the truth which is of paramount importance to us is that consciousness is an emergent value that arises at the human level and lends a unique glory to man as the focus of Being. It reveals to him the realm of boundless possibilities and makes him the master of his destiny. It bestows upon him the creative ability to refashion life and society into an image of his inner vision of truth and beauty and righteousness.

HISTORY

We are living in the twentieth century and we are citizens of the world. It is for us to be able to draw on the limitless wisdom of East and West and North and South. That is the great privilege of modern man. The cultural heritage of the entire human race is open to him. Wherever there is truth, wherever there is wisdom, we can freely draw upon it and bring it all together into a grand synthesis.

A. *THE MEANING OF HISTORY*

The full meaning of history can be disclosed only when it is studied in the context of evolution and as a mode of manifestation of the creativity of Being. Man's creativity is, in ultimate analysis, the creativity of Being continued on the human level of self-consciousness and value-consciousness.

Man is both a time-binder and a time-transcender. He transcends time in all manner of transpersonal experiences. He also surveys time as a stream continuously flowing from the past through the present toward the future. By casting his glance backward, he brings the past alive in history with a view to drawing freely from its accumulated wisdom. By binding together the past, present, and future, he participates in evolution as an agency for the creative urge of Being.

Since the past, present, and future interpenetrate and intermingle in the creativity of time, history can hardly be understood fully without reference to the planetary evolution, of which it is an integral part. Nor can it be adequately understood without reference to the full potential of man as a unique and creative center of Being.

History is the human phase of planetary evolution. Before the appearance of man, the natural order emerged out of the depths of Being through the unconscious creative energy of nature. History began when man appeared with his self-consciousness. With this, nature acquired a higher organ of self-expression. Man's reflections upon the advance of time and his reflections upon his own reflections immediately lifted evolutionary nature to a higher level, and added to it new dimensions of creativity.

The process of history may aptly be visualized as the on-going movement of the evolutionary world spirit. Throughout this process, a transition has taken place from the process of biological evolution to include that of psycho-social progress. There also has been a transition from the unconscious creativity of nature to the conscious expression of man's creative freedom. Be it noted, however, that with all his freedom, man is still part of nature, and both man and nature are always aspects of Being.

History is the working out of the inner light of Being guiding the self-conscious soul of man. The dynamic world spirit is seated in the car of evolution, in the process of fuller manifestation. The nontemporal aspect of Being guides the process of evolution from within. It is the supra-historical source of inspiration to the historical process.

Not all historians are agreed as to the precise meaning and goal of history. Has the march of history any ultimate goal as hinted above? Is it only the arena or stage on which various cultural systems and civilizations go through successive stages of birth, growth, decay, and death? If human evolution has any ultimate goal, is it within the power of man himself to reach that goal? Or, considering the predominance of the power drive and destructive impulse in man, and his success in inventing massive means of total destruction, is he destined to perish before reaching the full realization of his age-long dream and his potential? All kinds of answers have been given to the above questions. Let us have a quick glance at the views of some thinkers and historians of modern times.

Most historians are agreed that civilizations and cultures of various types are the basic intelligible units of the study of history. They are further agreed that a common characteristic of all civilizations is that they have a cyclical rise-growth-fall pattern, a birth-maturity-death pattern. They differ, however, as to the ultimate goal of the rise and fall of civilizations.

Oswald Spengler[1] thinks that every culture is like a macrocosmic organism. It has a distinctive soul, personality, style of its own. Inherent in every culture-soul is its destiny-idea

As a macrocosmic organism, every culture goes through the four seasons of Spring, Summer, Autumn, and Winter. The springtime of culture corresponds to the childhood of the human individual. It is the stage of unquestioning religious belief and fanciful and enchanting mythological insights. The Spring is followed by the Summer which corresponds to the youthful period of the human individual. This period is characterized by the appearance of a spirit of critique and reform, resulting in the development of metaphysical ideas. The Summer is followed by Autumn, when the cultural macrocosm reaches its full maturity. This is when reason comes to its own and plays a dominant role in all activities and self-expressions. Winter sees the dawn of materialism in its various forms as the ruling principle of social existence. People are either frankly skeptical or nihilistic, or they pay only lip-homage to higher cultural and spiritual values.

In Spengler's view, history is the morphological study of this cyclical process. He pessimistically viewed his own time as the decline phase or destiny-fulfillment phase of Western European culture. Every culture-soul has its own distinctive world-view—its unique art expression, knowledge formulation, and socio-political organization. This is a view of perfect cultural relativism. In his view, mankind has no aim, no idea, no plan any more than the family of butterflies or orchids. Instead of beholding world-history as the one linear history of the human race, Spengler pictures it as "the drama of a number of mighty Cultures", which "bloom and age as the oaks and the pines, the blossoms, twigs and leaves",[2] without there being any aging mankind.

Spengler's theory of cultural relativism and historical relativity stems from his failure to grasp the significance of some unique features of human evolution. Characteristic of the latter are the continuous processes of migration and intermarriage, and interracial, intercultural and international communication. Teilhard de Chardin has described the process as "convergent integration".[3] In consequence of this species-revolving and convergent integration, mankind is the only successful type which has remained as a single, interbreeding and self-integrating group of species.

The central fact of human evolution as a gradually self-integrating and self-enriching process of the entire human race is bound to change essentially our perspective of world history. It is not just the morphological study of a limited number of macrocosmic culture-organisms, self-contained and mutually non-communicative. On the contrary, it is the drama of constantly interacting cultures and civilizations eventuating in the evolutionary advance of mankind as a whole.

What then is the ultimate goal of world history? What is the secret purpose and destiny, if any, of the evolutionary advance of mankind as a whole?

I think the most rigorous self-discipline is necessary to suggest an answer to this question. The question of goal, meaning, purpose, or destiny is not a matter of some actual fact to observe. It cannot be settled with reference to some incontrovertible data of perception. It calls for penetrative insight and creative imagination, which are more subjective in texture than objective. Precisely for that reason there is abundant room here for wishful thinking, for subjective coloration, for the secret operation of one's racial, religious, cultural, or ideological predilection.

Hegel,[4] as an idealist, contemplates world history as the dialectical progression of ideas unfolding through the triadic rhythm of thesis, antithesis, and synthesis. The ultimate goal of this dialectical march of ideas is the determinate formulation of one all-comprehensive grand synthesis of ideas, absolute and final. And that, of course, is his own philosophy of absolute idealism.

In terms of socio-political conditions, according to Hegel, history begins in Asia with the childlike "unreflected consciousness" of the Absolute laying the foundation for absolute emperorship. The second stage, the adolescence of the Absolute, is represented by the Greek world where the free spirit of rational inquiry begins and the democratic ideal is born. The third stage, the manhood of the Absolute, is manifested in the Roman world where the State in its abstract universality becomes important and individuals, whose rights are recognized, sacrifice them for national welfare. The fourth and final stage of history is reached in the German world where all men are recognized as free men and they freely identify their best interests with the integrity and welfare of the German State. And thus, for Hegel, the concrete manifestation of the Absolute Idea can be provided only by the German State, which represents the final embodiment of the historical dialectic.

Drawing inspiration from Hegel, Karl Marx[5] also envisions history as the one-cycle dialectical movement of progress toward the complete realization of freedom in human society. However, he replaces Hegel's idealistic interpretation with his own materialistic interpretation of history. The historical process is, in his view, determined by the conflict of class interests in regard to the means of production and distribution of social wealth. History advances through the various stages of primitive communism, slavery, feudalism, and capitalism, and culminates in the classless society of scientific communism.

It should be evident to all who reflect that both the Hegelian and the Marxian interpretations of history are colored by the Western European cultural provincialism of their authors. Both absolute idealism and dialectical materialism are fruits of Western European culture, the first representing the interests of the German middle class, and the latter representing the interests of the factory workers of the military-industrial complex of Western Europe.

Spengler saw through the cultural provincialism of parochialism of such ideological interpretations of history. His own approach, therefore, was in an important sense a Copernican discovery in the historical sphere. He resolutely refused to set up the value system of a particular culture as the absolute standard of historical judgment. In surveying and appreciating the various cultures and dynamic components of the drama of history, he courageously took his stand outside of them all in a transcendent realm of pure thought. It is unfortunate that he eventually swung to the opposite extreme and landed in extreme cultural relativism, losing sight of the evolutionary creative impulse of life as the ultimate datum of experience and the absolute of thought.

Arnold J. Toynbee[6] agrees with Spengler that cultures and civilizations are the ultimate intelligible units of historical study. He also agrees that all civilizations share the same fate of rise-and-fall, going through the four stages of genesis, growth, breakdown, and eventual disintegration. Toynbee, however, is emphatic in his belief that running through all the perishing civilizations, the chariot of history marches forward developing higher religions which alone, in his view, constitute the ultimate hope and salvation of mankind. Civilizations are merely handmaids to the march of history from glory to glory.

Even though Toynbee admits that God or Truth is not the monopoly of any particular religion and that all the four higher religions living today, such as Christianity, Islam, Mahayana Buddhism, and Hinduism, express the glory of God as Love in various ways, he eventually accords a preeminent position to Christianity. He envisages the ultimate goal of history as the unification of the world around the true social gospel of Christianity.

Thus, Toynbee's theological interpretation of history eventually ends up with a parochial slant, the unconscious religious bias assuming the upper hand. As Professor Albert William Levi points out, in the last five volumes of Toynbee's *A Study of History*, he gives up his empirical approach, and his Christian bias and parochialism overcome him. He envisions the path of history as "the path of messianic Christianity into Augustine's *Civitas Dei*".[8]

At this point, we encounter the most crucial problem of the philosophy of history. A purely empirical approach necessarily ends up with the denial of any meaning, any plot, or predetermined pattern to history. History is reduced to just the playground of the contingent and the unforeseen, a meaningless welter of chaotic detail, a brute succession of chance happenings.

On the other hand, a speculative approach affirming the validity of a meaningful philosophy of history, more often than not, gives rein to the projective mechanism of the philosopher's mind. A philosopher sharing the factory worker's hatred of the capitalist management naturally wishes to see the goal of history as a classless society controlled by the workingmen. A philosopher identified with a particular race believed to be the master race of the world, loves to envision the goal of history as a benevolent dictatorship in which the whole world is piously ruled by God's chosen race. A philosopher identified with a particular religion secretly aspires to behold the goal of history as the glorious fulfillment of his religion's dream of the City of God or the Kingdom of Heaven.

Then again, a philosopher fascinated by a certain analogy, such as the analogy of the living organism applied to human culture is inclined to carry that analogy lopsidedly too far and contemplate history as the blooming and bursting of various macrocosmic culture organisms.

Let us, therefore, set aside for a moment all analogies and metaphors, all poetry and imagination. Let us set aside all speculative structures of meaning created by wishful thinking. Man with all his self-consciousness and relative freedom is essentially an integral part of nature. So, it would be reasonable to suppose that the meaning of history is part of the meaning of all creation and evolution. It lies in the endlessly diversified manifestation of the boundless creativity of Being.

Since the creative energy of Being is inexhaustible, we can hardly imagine any final and full stop to the creative process, whether evolutionary or historical. No order of creation, no culmination of evolutionary endeavor, no achievement of historical striving, can be the last word of this process. By the very nature of the case, nothing incarnate in space-time can be equated with the infinite and eternal Being.

B. *THE LAW OF COSMIC BALANCE*

The law of karma, or cosmic balance, was perceived by the sages of India, including Gautama Buddha, as the most fundamental law of cosmic significance. It was affirmed as the law of all laws insofar as all other laws of life and existence can be derived from it.

However, on the popular level, this law has received many narrow interpretations and misleading practical applications. For instance, one misinterpretation has induced people to be fatalistic in outlook. In point of truth, the law of cosmic balance is the most well-known vindication of the intrinsic freedom of man. It means that the situation in which man finds himself today is the outcome of his own actions freely performed in the past; but he has always the built-in ability to rise above the past and freely initiate new courses of action. By virtue of free actions performed in the living present, he creatively advances into the future and thus functions as the architect of his own destiny.

Another popular misinterpretation induces some people to be indifferent or apathetic to the sufferings of other people and withdraw into the shell of excessive self-concern and personal liberation. However, the truth is just the opposite. The law of cosmic balance implies the spiritual imperative of universal compassion so that by helping and loving one another we can enhance and strengthen our good karma as a potent force in attaining enlightenment and cosmo-centric living.

A third major misinterpretation is the ancient Indian version of the ancient theological doctrine of Divine predetermination of Kismet, or of the ancient Greek tragic view of supernatural Kairos, or of the modern Freudian view of unconscious psychological determinism. Properly understood, the law of cosmic balance contemplates the advance of life as a dynamic interaction between the force of personal ethical determinism as well as the dynamic presence of the eternally free spirit in man.

All the aforesaid misinterpretations of the law of cosmic balance stem from failure to grasp the ultimate philosophical significance of the law. It is an irony of history that the highest spiritual law of life became a source of justification for all manner of unspiritual behavior.

Formulated in purely philosophical terms the law of cosmic balance means that the universe in its wholeness is a harmonious structure, a self-coherent whole, a self-adjusting and self-preserving system. Whenever the harmony of the whole is disturbed through any change or conflict, any upheaval or catastrophe, any novelty or fresh development, the universe maintains its over-ruling harmony by producing a counter change or counter movement of energy. The cosmic whole is thus in its essential structure the supreme self-sustaining, self-regulating and self-fulfilling system.

It is because the macroscomic universe is a self-adjusting and self-regulating system that man, the microcosm, who is an image of the cosmic infinite, is also a self-adjusting system in miniature. Nowadays we have cybernetics as the science of small self-adjusting systems like servo-mechanisms and living organisms governed by the law of self-adjusting balance. Viewed from the scientific standpoint, the law of cosmic balance may be defined as the macro-cybernetic law of cosmic nature.

What is the ultimate support or ground of the law of cosmic balance? What is the nature of the power that upholds this supreme law whose sovereign authority prevails over all existence?

This is an ultimate metaphysical question, a perennial problem of philosophy. Who can conclusively solve this greatest riddle of the universe? Different philosophers and sages, differenet thinkers and spiritual masters, according to their personal temperament and life-experience, or in response to their historic mission or mankind's evolutionary condition, present different versions of the ultimate cosmic riddle.

Some think that the law of cosmic balance is sustained by the all-powerful, all-wise and all-good personal God. Some visualize this divine power as the supernatural Heavenly Father; some again visualize the same as the all-pervasive Divine Mother. Some contemplate the supreme spirit that sustains the cosmic harmony as the transcendent unknowable Godhead; some again perceive the Supreme as the all-pervasive Presence accessible to mystic realization. Some affirm the absolute spirit as the all-encompassing cosmic consciousness; some again prefer to designate the Supreme as pure existence-consciousness-bliss.

Theological debates and metaphysical discussions regarding the ultimate cosmic riddle have proved interminable in history. Still under the irresistable compulsion of some fundamental psychic need, different people have felt it necessary to accept on faith this or that particular theological, metaphysical or mystical answer to the great riddle as the pivot of their own personal balance in life. This is all very fine. The only problem is that such unverifiable articles of fatih, instead of unifying the collective life of mankind, have proved as powerful divisive forces. That is why the need was felt in modern times to organize the collective living of organized societies on the basis of secular humanism, setting religious differences to the side.

But what about the spiritual life of man? How can mankind be unified on the spiritual level and inspired to fulfill the destiny of human existence on earth by establishing the kingdom of truth, love and peace?

By exploring the spiritual heritage of India we come up with two answers to the above question. Either of these answers, practiced as the ontological root of the law of cosmic balance, can solve the problem of human unity and guide us toward a peaceful global society. These two answers are hidden in the two pivotal concepts of Brahman and Dharma, which have been the mainsprings of inspiration of Hinduism and Buddhism respectively.

According to the philosophical tradition of Hinduism, the ontological root of the law of cosmic balance is to be found in the mystery of indeterminable Being which different religions call by different names. On the basis of this spiritual understanding, peoples from all parts of the world, regardless of their divergent religious, metaphysical and ideological backgrounds, can join hands in the spirit of full cooperation in the name of one supreme Godhead of diverse names and for the sake of the ultimate good of humanity as a whole.

According to the most austere philosophical tradition of Buddhism, the concept of God, an intellectual construction, or an unverifiable product of human speculation, is like a signal for the opening of Pandora's Box. As soon as we open the Box the atmosphere is smoke-filled with all manner of conflicting theological, metaphysical, and mystical ideas without any end in sight and with a blinding effect on our vision of the ultimate goal of human unity and love. So as the world's first spiritual scientist, Buddha cut out the lure of theological and metaphysical speculation. He decided to present the law of cosmic balance as an expression of the essential structure of the universe. The eternal truth, or *dharma*, reflects that essential structure. To raise any further question about the cause of that structure or about the support of the supreme law is both an illegitimate question, and an exercise in futility. It is an illegitimate question because the law of cause and effect is applicable only to the finite things and phenomena, not to the infinite universe as a whole. It is an exercise in futility, because whatever ultimate cause is postulated in explanation of the universe as a whole would require another cause, and that again another cause, and so on endlessly, generating an infinite regress. It is a question uttered by immature thinking. Moreover, whatever transcendent self-sufficient cause might be postulated would be beyond all verification and therefore beyond all chances of human agreement. So one should understand the law of cosmic balance as inseparably one with the ultimate structure of the universe, just as in modern science the laws of gravity and relativity, etc., are understood as phenomenological descriptions of the structure of the universe.

From the standpoint of man's social existence or moral consciousness, the cosmic balance appears as the ethical order of the universe, just as from the standpoint of man's intellect or rational consciousness it appears as a perfectly intelligible scheme. Einstein contemplated with awe and admiration the grandeur or reason incarnate in nature. The Upanishadic sages of India perceived that the power of Truth, or cosmic law (Satyam), that controls the operations of nature is inseparably one with the power of justice (Ritam), which ldetermines the destinies of civilized man. They called it Satyam Ritam Vrihat, or the comprehensive Truth-Justice. In the same way Immanuel Kant intuitively sensed the indivisible unity of "the starry heavens above" and the "moral law within".

The law of cosmic balance—or karma—as an expression of the ethical order of the universe is variously articulated in many neat formulas: as you sow, so you reap; hatred begets hatred, violence provokes violence; love awakens love; kindness evokes kindness. All these are a reflection on the ethical level of human existence of the same law operative on the physical level such as: every action has an equal and opposite reaction; every particle of matter (or proton) provokes a counter-particle (or electron); every movement of energy in a definite direction (entropy, or dissipation of energy) is balanced by an opposite movement of energy (or negative entropy, that is, a creative rechanneling of energy).

The same universal law is operative in the realm of evolution in the principle of the dialectic. Every thesis or positive force of evolution is balanced in the creative flux of time by a counter movement or antithesis. The resulting opposition generates the energy for a higher synthesis or balanced unity of opposites. In the realm of thinking, for instance, we understand matter best by contrasting it with mind, the opposite of matter. Then our perception of the opposition of matter impels us by an immanent dialectic, as Hegel would say, beyond both matter and mind into the higher synthesis of spirit or unifying comprehensive consciousness of both matter and mind. Turning to the arena of man's socio-political evolution we find that every political party provokes into existence an opposite party so that in the course of social progress a healthy balance of opposite forces is maintained.

Let us take note here of a deeeper refinement of the law of cosmic balance which supervenes at the human stage of evolution. At the beginning this law was expressed in a crude form such as "an eye for an eye, a tooth for a tooth". This gives rise to the social condition in which "he who lives by the sword perishes by the sword" or "he who decapitates a person shall receive capital punishment". The self-adjusting and balancing power of the social organism is pretty well reflected here in the motto "tit for tat". But at a higher phase of evolution of mankind—the phase which is regretably still more of a dream than a reality—the balancing power of civilization may lie in the application of a profoundly superior kind of force such as the alchemy of the soul force.

As a spiritual being, fully evolved man has the intrinsic ability to destroy social imbalance not through violent annihilation but by application of the spirit's transforming power of love and understanding, sacrifice and compassion. When out of the fullness of understanding and compassion, you turn the other cheek to your enemy, his heart is likely to melt in bewildered self-repentence. The deepest chord of his soul is likely to vibrate in unison with the higher law of life of which he catches a faint glimpse. The efficacy of love as a superior self-adjusting power of the cosmic balance is gloriously illustrated in the life stories of such embodiments of the creative soul of cosmic evolution as Gautama and Jesus, Schweitzer and Gandhi. It is through institutionalization of this superior power of spiritual transformation that our society may one day succeed in abolishing the torture chambers and capital punishment devices of our current dispensation of criminal justice.

From the perspective of international politics the cosmic balance is perceived as the balance of international justice. It is the harmony of international relations conducive to the independent growth and willing cooperation of all the nations, peoples and states of the world.

It is because the law of cosmic balance is operative in mankind's collective and international life that we find empires built upon sheer violence and brute force are eventually swept away by the irresistable tides of history. "He who lives by the sword perishes by the sword" or "the slayer is eventually slain by his counternumber" is no less true in international relations than in interpersonal relations.

As sure as broad daylight, ruthless despots and dictators eventually perish in ignominy by the swift retribution of justice. He who takes delight in war as a power game is bound to succumb to the poisonous fumes of war as the death dance of destiny. The same benign goodness which is Shiva is also the devastating death blow of Rudra. Love and death, eros and thanatos, are two faces of the same reality, the law of cosmic balance, the self-adjusting power of harmony.

Man, in his ignorance, frequently misperceives the international order of justice as the balance of brute force or as the balance or terror euphemistically called the political balance of the state system. In the name of the political balance of power, mightier nations make designs to dominate and exploit weaker nations. Antagonistic power blocks are created and a competitive arms race is unleashed to satisfy the insatiable will to power. Fanciful ideologies are invented to justify and legitimize or rationalize the unconscious power drive. The hypnotic spell of ignorance (or *maya*) is so strong that all this power craze is pursued under the tantalizing illusion of achieving peace through destruction, freedom through domination, and welfare through exploitation. The result is the perpetuation of the vicious cycle of ceaseless suffering sustained by the invisible chords of primal nescience.

There is only one way out of this dangerous vicious cycle in which the human race is enmeshed due to the self-spun cobwebs of *maya*. The all-conquering light of truth, justice and love alone shatters the death trap of dark cobwebs. The great need of our times is the need for world statesmen with a global outlook and with a keen perception of the indivisible unity of the destinies of all nations. So the law of cosmic balance in international relations means the balance of justice is an essential factor in optimum human evolution on earth. Translated into political language it means the balance of power, perspective and plurality. At the present stage of human evolution when the death instinct or destructive impulses are still very predominant in human nature the time is not yet ripe for complete abolition of military power and strategy. Since the will to power is still an essential ingredient of the human will, the absence of military strength is more often than not misconstrued as weakness and consequently serves as an open invitation to aggressive and exploitative nations. We know how in interpersonal relations those who are naively good and sentimentally sweet become helpless victims of the power-hungry self-seekers. The same is true in international relations, only a thousand times more so. Herein lies the wisdom of the great American President, Theodore Roosevelt's maxim: "Speak softly but carry a big stick."

But a clear vision of the ultimate humanistic goal calls for the use of the big stick always with utmost caution, with calm calculation of the pros and cons, with humanistic concern for the legitimate rights and liberties of all the peoples and nations of the world.

The right and intelligent use of power requires then a global perspective permeated by authentic humanistic concern. Power without perspective is a self-defeating disturbance of the global balance. Sooner or later it is likely to recoil upon the thoughtless wielder of power like a poisonous boomerang. This is how the law of cosmic balance operates on the power level.

The right perspective within international relations in its turn demands graceful acceptance of plurality as a real and legitimate manifestation of the creative unity of life. History is a record of repeated failures of desperate efforts to achieve large scale human unity by crushing pluralities into the shadow of abject death and domination. The monochromatic strategy has been tried with the help of an all-mighty emperor, with the help of one religious creed, and finally with the help of one universal ideology. The transparent lesson of history is that it is plurality in unity which holds the ultimate meaning of life and civilization. The right humanistic perspective implies an enlightened recognition of the legitimate existence and evolutionary significance of the different creeds and ideologies as well as of the different peoples, races and nations of the world. To set up one creed or ideology in a monotheistic crusading spirit with fanatical zeal is a sure way to face the music of an equally fanatical and crusading creed or ideology. This is how the law of cosmic balance operates on the conceptual or ideological level.

The law of cosmic balance as the law of international balance and harmony is therefore the law of power, perspective and plurality.

When applied in the sphere of man's spiritual evolution, the law of cosmic balance gives rise to the doctrine of reincarnation. It means that the indwelling spirit of every human individual is engaged in a long process of evolution toward the attainment of his ultimate destiny, namely, the full flowering of the human potential variously described as self-realization, God-realization, Being-cognition, self-actualization, etc. But few individuals can achieve this ultimate goal in one lifetime.

It is absolutely contrary to our faith in cosmic justice to accept the phenomenon of death as ultimate reality. After a long hard struggle a person succeeds in taking a few steps forward toward his spiritual destiny. He is just beginning to gain a clear vision of his goal and to profit by the mistakes and failures of his past. He is just beginning to emerge slowly from the slumber of the flesh and from the dark night of his original alienation from Being. If, right at that moment, in the midst of the new dawn's rich promise, his life is cut short by the cruel hand of death, would not cosmic justice immediately turn to abysmal absurdity? Would not our sense of higher justice be immediately reduced to a cruel joke perpetrated by some cosmic monster? Or should we in the final analysis accept the world as intrinsically beyond all meaning and therefore no more than a senseless flux of becoming, a curious blend of existentialist rebellion and surrealistic painting?

It has been noted before that the law of cosmic balance affirms the conservation of all values as well as the conservation of energy. It affirms the reality of balance and harmony in the emergence of divergent forms and values as well as in the interaction of multitudinous forces and events.

This means that all the precious values mankind gains, whether individually or collectively, are preserved in the collective unconscious or the universal life force which serves as the sustaining medium of evolution. Exactly what form and to what extent this preservation of evolutionary gains assumes is understandably an extremely controversial issue. It permits a whole spectrum of diversified opinions with extreme scepticism of any individual spiritual survival, to continuation of the individual soul as an essentially imperishable spiritual entity.

The truth probably lies midway between the two extremes. The voice of wisdom counsels the futility of excessive speculation about post-mortem existence. The imperative of life is to focus on the living present, to concentrate on a reasonable span of the present life with all its challenges and opportunities, with all its glories and frustrations, with all its rights and responsibilities, with all its dark nights of despair and bright days of creative achievement.

Active participation in the living present creatively advances into a glorious future.

PSYCHOLOGY

We so often lay emphasis upon perfecting our institutions. Much of our emphasis is on the external machinery. It is important to realize that without a radical change of heart, of inner consciousness, no matter how perfect the machinery is, things cannot radically change. After all, it is man who is going to operate the machinery.

A. INTEGRAL PSYCHOLOGY

Integral psychology is based upon experiences and insights affirming the multi-dimensional richness and indivisible wholeness of human personality. It is founded upon the concept of man's total self as the integral unity of uniqueness, relatedness, and transcendence, as the indivisible unity of the existential and the transcendental.

The basic insights of integral psychology can be set forth in the form of the following tenets:
- The individual is a body-mind-spirit continuum.
- All forms of experience must be taken into account.
- Thoroughly integrated consciousness is the profoundest potential of man.
- Higher levels of consciousness reveal dimensions of reality beyond the apprehension of ordinary mental and conceptual levels.
- There is an urge to self-expression in creative union with Being.
- Transformation of personality is the goal of personal development.

Let us now briefly elucidate the aforesaid salient features of integral psychology.

Wholeness of Personality

Integral psychology rejects the dichotomy of body and mind with which Western psychology has had to deal. Rene Descartes developed a dualistic outlook by driving a wedge between body and mind. He considered them absolutely heterogeneous substances *toto caelo* different from each other. Matter has extension as its essential attribute but no consciousness; mind has consciousness as its essential attribute but no consciousness; mind has consciousness as its essential attribute but no extension in space. This unmitigated dualism of matter and mind creates the problem of mind-body interaction.

In Indian psychology the same kind of problem did not arise. In traditional yoga psychology both mind and body are regarded as evolutes or different forms of manifestation of the same creative energy, which is characterized by some kind of imminent finality or purposiveness. So, mind and body, as divergent energy-formations, can act and react upon each other without any difficulty.

But in the traditional yoga psychology of Patanjali, the spirit *(purusha)*, the principle of pure egoless consciousness, is postulated as essentially and radically different from energy *(prakriti)*, which is manifest as the body-mind continuum. The spirit or self is immutable, immobile, eternally perfect. In consequence, it is intrinsically indifferent[1] to the affairs of the world, to profit and loss, pains and pleasures, comedies, and tragedies. It is only through self-oblivion that the spirit is induced, in the form of the empirical self, to participate in the game of life. As soon as restored to its original essence through self-realization, it shines in its intrinsic glory, in utter indifference to the cosmic dance of *prakriti*.

In integral psychology this traditional yogic dichotomy of spirit and nature or energy is also transcended. There is no existential separation between them. Nature, as energy, is nothing but the creativity of spirit. Spirit and nature are one,[2] just as the being of fire and the burning capacity of fire are one. Physical motion, life force, psychic energy, etc., are different forms of expression of the same fundamental energy, which is capable of producing infinite diversities of form and quality, existence and value. The same energy which creates body and mind, does also give rise to man's egoless consciousness, global perspective, transcendental awareness, etc. In the present writer's interpretation, the latter are emergent values supervening upon the optimum functioning of man's nervous system crowned with the brain. It follows from this view that the human personality is a body-mind-spirit continuum, a nature-spirit whole.

The Importance of all Phases
and Areas of Experience

In the yoga psychology of India, four fundamental phases of human experience are recognized: waking, dream, deep sleep, and samadhi or transpersonal experience. First, during waking hours we have the preceptual experience of the world around us, of the multitudinous objects constantly impinging upon our sense organs. Second, we have different kinds of dream experience. Dreams represent not only imaginary fulfillment of suppressed wishes and inchoate fears, they also represent many extra-sensory perceptions including clairvoyance, clairaudience, precognitions of the future, prophetic visions of one's own destiny, etc. Third, there is deep dreamless sleep, which upon close inspection discloses some kind of ever-awake consciousness in man. In deep sleep the conscious rational mind is no doubt put to rest so that the body can relax and recuperate, but a deeper level of detached, passive objectless and onlooker type of consciousness is found to exist. Fourth, there is the fourth-dimensional transcendental experience. It is transpersonal experience of the ultimate ground of one's own being, or the Self in its suchness. This is a very blissful experience of transcendence variously known as *samadhi, bodhi, satori, jnana, prajna,* etc.

In traditional yoga psychology, ontological primacy is given to the experience of *samadhi* or transcendental self-realization. As a result, the Self or Spirit, or pure transcendental consciousness alone is considered ultimately real. Other experiences involving body and mind are supposed to belong to the realm of ignorance, or the not-self. The body and the mind are believed to be radically different from, outside of, and therefore alien to, the true Self.

Integral psychology has a somewhat different conception. All the above-mentioned phases of experience reveal in our view equally real aspects of human personality. But the physical, the instinctual and the mental are no less important components of the total self than the spiritual and the transcendental. Transcendental consciousness may be more fundamental, more luminous, more revelatory of the structure of reality, but it certainly is not the only reality of the only value that counts. Physical consciousness or body awareness, instinctual drives, reason, and the I-sense (i.e., the sense of individuality), freedom of choice, participation in the creativity of life, etc., are equally real constituents of the total self. There can be no perfect self-realization without the actualization of the physical, emotional, intellectual, social and spiritual potentialities of man.

The Concept of Integral Self-Realization

Integral psychology is dominated by the concept of integral self-realization as the ultimate goal of personality growth. Integral self-realization implies freedom from all inner conflicts and tensions, full flowering of one's independent personality, and awareness of one's transcendent Self as the unitive consciousness of the cosmic whole.

Modern depth psychology has called attention to the paramount need of bridging the gulf between the conscious mind and the unconscious. The conscious rational mind must come to terms with the seemingly irrational unconscious. As the contents and forces of the unconscious are brought to light and accepted as part of one's own being and incorporated into the growing and expanding personality, a new center of consciousness emerges. Dr. C. G. Jung aptly describes it as the individuation process. It is the integration of personality harmonizing the conscious and unconscious components of the psyche.

In modern existentialist philosophy emphasis is upon freedom as the essential structure of the self. The dominating conception is that of self-existence, which is realized through the three stages of assimilation, independence, and creativity. Frederic Nietzsche has described these three stages as three successive metamorphoses of the spirit in man: the camel, the lion, and the child.[3]

Every human being is born in a certain socio-cultural context and at a certain point of history. He has to draw upon and assimilate the cultural heritage of his own country, and if possible, of the entire human race. This is what Nietzsche calls the camel stage. The camel has the power of storing up in his body enormous amounts of food and water for his arduous journey across the desert. Likewise the individual man has to store up in his memory the accumulated wisdom of the past as an aid to his personal search for the truth.

In the course of his personal development the time comes when the camel is suddenly metamorphosed into the lion. The lion proceeds to tear apart the huge monster known as "thou shalt not". The lion in man, his free spirit of individuality, roars against the supposedly sacrosanct inviolability of social authority—the authority of scriptural injunctions, divine commandments, political edicts, religious dogmas and creeds, etc. The individual now discovers his own inner light as the ultimate source of all authentic values. He becomes aware of his primary obligation to his own inner creativity, to his inmost hidden potential.

The awareness of one's own dynamic potential brings in its train a spirit of humility and a profound concern. A new sense of purpose and personal mission begins to dawn upon the mind. The individual feels that he is pregnant with a new baby, a new style of life, a new mode of self-expression. That is when the lion is suddenly metamorphosed into a child.

The above is a fine description of the concept of self-existence as the discovery of one's own dynamic potentials and the free choice of one's purpose and style of living. But it fails to take into account the other—no less important—aspect of human reality, namely, his essential relatedness to the cosmic whole, his rootedness in Being as the ground of the universe. A person may be enamored of the glory of his self-existence to such an extent that he may wish to see the whole world as a mere reflection of his own image. He may place himself on a pedestal for all mankind to worship. There is no guarantee against the Nietzschean superman abusing his power for the enslavement of the human race or violation of his basic psycho-social relationship.

Whereas the ideal of self-existence ignores the reality of transcendence in life, the ideal of transcendental self-realization, on the other hand, fails to grasp the dynamic significance of the individual's existence or being-in-the-world. An individual may attain perfect independence and freedom, but he cannot gain wholeness of being without realizing his position as a dynamic component of human evolution. An individual may experience the joy of boundless self-expansion by realizing his oneness with the cosmic whole, but transcendence has to be further transcended. For wholeness of being one must appreciate the unique value of his individuality as a creative spark, as a set of dynamic potentials to be actualized for the good of society. A dynamic balance has to be established between the individual and the transcendental poles of one's total being.

Individuation implies emancipation from all inner conflicts and divisions. Transcendental self-realization implies transpersonal experience of Being. It is the realization of one's basic identity as an integral part of the cosmic whole. This realization gives rise to the spirit of universal love and genuine concern for cosmic welfare. The concept of integral self-realization implies the unity of individuation, on the one hand, and free self-giving for the common welfare of mankind, on the other. It is the unity of individual freedom and universal love.

Different Levels of Consciousness

Self-realization can be described as an adventure of consciousness. When in the course of transcendence the conscious rational mind is reduced to nothingness, the light of the unknown begins to beckon. Hidden realms of the unconscious and the superconscious begin to loom large. New insights into the depths of existence and new vistas of thought begin to emerge.

The mind is often clouded by ignorance. Ignorance consists in seeing things in their isolation and separateness rather than in their wholeness and interrelatedness. For instance, when an individual perceives himself as a separate entity existing independently of the environment or the cosmic whole, the result is an isolated and separative consciousness. In the course of the inner growth of consciousness the veil of ignorance begins to be lifted, the barriers of separation begin to break, the boundaries of the mind recede, and one experiences an increasing expansion of consciousness.

Eventually one may leap forth beyond the furthest boundaries of the mind. He discovers what has been called pure transcendental consciousness. This is the no-mind, no-ego, nondual type of consciousness. On its discovery one has the experience of transcending space, time and causation, and also soaring beyond all names and forms, all images and ideas. It is the experience not so much of mind-expansion as of mind- and ego-annihilation, resulting in the discovery of a radically new dimension of Being. Transcendental consciousness is perfectly egoless awareness of reality in its indivisible unity. It is the awareness of reality on the silent non-verbal level—non-conceptual and non-dichotomizing.

As a result of newly emergent levels of consciousness, intensified and expanded, one is precipitated into radically new dimensions, just as under the pressure of heat, water turns into steam. These new dimensions of consciousness represent actualization of the human potential. They represent wider perspectives on the nature of existence and deeper insights into the mystery of Being.

Ontomotivation

Abraham Maslow has introduced in modern Western psychology the concept of metamotivation. He rightly points out that besides such basic deficiency needs as the need for food and shelter, for safety and security, for love and approval, there is the metaneed, the growth impulse in man. It is the need to outgrow expediency and egocentricity and to know things as they are apart from their usefulness or harmfulness to us. It is the need to appreciate and express such intrinsic values as truth, beauty, justice, harmony, freedom, etc. When a man is dedicated to such values for their own sake, he is metamotivated. As he puts it, people who are reasonably gratified in their basic needs become metamotivated by the intrinsic values of Being (B-values, as he calls them).[4]

Maslow is expressing here a very profound insight into the motivational dynamics of the human psyche. Integral psychology carries this analysis a little further. The growth impulse in man reaches its highest fulfillment when he becomes non-conceptually aware of Being as the ultimate ground of his own existence. It is known as the fourth dimensional or transcendental awareness. It represents a revolutionary change in consciousness, a radically different dimension of awareness. It is like the flower suddenly bursting into bloom, or like the sun suddenly emerging in all its effulgence out of the thick veil of clouds.

As a result of this experience, a flood of light is thrown upon different parts of the unconscious psyche. The barrier between the conscious and the unconscious breaks down. Unresolved conflicts and hidden motivations are laid bare. Selfish impulses and ego drives are burnt to ashes. In consequence, a person—at least for some time—feels completely detached from the world and disinterested in any kind of action, because all familiar motivations are now gone.

But as the awareness of Being matures further, Being is perceived as inseparable from becoming. Reality is perceived as inseparable from creativity. Life is perceived as inseparable from self-expressive energy. Being in its integral fullness is perceived as logos-eros, wisdom-creativity, consciousness-energy. The individual self, having identified with Being, now becomes one with the creative energy of Being. Integral experience of Being transforms him into a creative personality. This gives rise to a new kind of motivation, the motivation of dynamic oneness or creative fellowship with Being. It is the kind of motivation which transcends all instinctual drives of the unconscious. It also transcends all previous ideas about truth, beauty, justice, peace, freedom, etc. A person is truly reborn. His sense of values undergoes a radical change, a total transvaluation. His vision of truth and beauty becomes one with the spirit of love liberated from the bonds of the ego. I suggest the designation of ontomotivation for such free and illumined oneness with the creativity of Being. One is now united with the superconscient dynamism of Being.

Transformation

The psychology of traditional mysticism is based upon the dichotomy of the flesh and the spirit. It is based upon the trenchant distinction between the natural and the supernatural, the lower self and the higher Self. Whereas the Western mystic has tried to save his soul by mortifying the flesh, the traditional yogi has tried to realize the Self by practicing austerities and following the path of ascetic renunciation.

Integral psychology recognizes the folly of both extreme puritanism and extreme asceticism. The total self is the unity of the empirical and the transcendental, the natural and the supernatural. It is the body-mind-spirit continuum, the energy consciousness continuum. The suppression of instincts, impulses and desires is a policy of self-mutilation. One may be alienated from the natural world. Whereas the instinctual man suffers from the sense of alienation from the higher self, the other worldly man contemptuous of the mortal coils suffers from the sense of alienation from the body and the natural order.

Traditional spirituality recommends a detour, a side-tracking of reason. The path of reason is indeed arduous self-discipline. It involves the prodigious strain of independent thinking and critical evaluation of conventional norms and values including religious dogmas and mystical paradoxes. To smother the voice of reason is no less a form of self-mutilation than instinctual starvation on one end and spiritual blindness at the other.

The reason why traditional spirituality is eager to bypass reason is that in its lower form 'intellect' or 'conceptual understanding' has a tendency to get caught in a network of its own concepts and categories. Intellect operates with such fixed categories as substance/quality, cause/effect, one/many, etc. It is inclined to attach ultimate significance to such trenchant distinctions or dichotomies as God and world, nature and spirit, flesh and soul, etc. Pretty soon it forgets the limitations of its fixed molds and the relativity of its polarities. Intuitive apprehension of reality reveals the unity underlying all conceptual divisions and the mystery transcending all conceptualizations.

But to admit that the conceptual understanding is inadequate to the concrete fullness of reality does not amount to recommending that the former must be bypassed or abandoned in our search for reality. Our concepts and categories are like finger-pointing to the light of truth. By no means to be construed as the equivalent of truth, they are nonetheless essential for our looking in the right direction. They are also essential for the sharing of valuable insights with our fellow beings.

Reason in its authentic essence is ontological thinking. It is an organ of articulation of the essential structure of reality. The basic allegiance of pure reason is to truth and reality, and not to practical usefulness and efficiency. It is not calculation of the chances of wish-fulfillment, but the elaboration and interpretation of experience in the quest of truth. With its gaze fixed upon truth, it institutes a constant criticism of categories, a perpetual re-examination of accepted notions and theories, an untiring reevaluation of all established values. Reason, in its higher form, is indeed the sworn enemy of all fixed ideas and frozen dogmas. It is a resolute refusal to be entrapped in the trenchant distinctions and irreconcilable oppositions of the intellect, which as a pragmatic function of the mind loses sight of the wholeness of reality.

Man as a thinking animal can never completely escape from thinking or reasoning. Mystic experiences such as *samadhi* or unitive consciousness are often asserted to be entirely beyond the rational. But on closer examination it will be found that there is an element of rationality in all authentic mystic experiences. When one leaves behind all logical notions and makes a direct encounter with reality, he perceives his experience to be supremely real and revelatory of the ultimate. In other words, the categories of reality and value are unmistakably inherent in his experience. He has transcended only the dichotomies of Aristotelian logic but not the evaluative affirmation of logos proper.

Since thought is co-extensive with experience, it is foolish to talk of suppressing or eliminating it. To bypass intellect or to leave it untutored and undisciplined in one's search for truth is to court self-mutilation or lopsided growth. Such a simplistic approach is likely to lead to excessive emotionalism or dogmatism. To abandon reason in the name of simple faith or absolutely immediate experience is to fall a victim to unconscious rationalization. The dynamics of human growth demands the development of reason to the fullest extent.

So, in the scheme of self-development as outlined in integral psychology, thought is accorded its legitimate place and function. It should not be neglected, suppressed or bypassed. Nor, on the other hand, should it be over-emphasized to the neglect of emotion, intuition, sensory apprehension and supersensuous Being-awareness. As Sri Aurobindo says, "Reason was the helper; reason is the bar."[5] Reason becomes a bar when an intellectual system, however monumental, is affirmed to be the whole of reality, or when the fixed molds and categories of the intellect are allowed to dictate to reality. But reason functions as an invaluable and indispensable aid to the continuous growth of human wisdom when it is allowed to coordinate, harmonize, interpret, and evaluate different areas and modes of human experience with a radical openness to ever new discoveries of experiential data.

The same principle of "transformation, not suppression", or of balanced affirmation, applies to all other aspects or functions of our personality. For instance, the body is not to be regarded as an impediment to spiritual growth or as a prison-house to be abandoned on the attainment of spiritual liberation. On the contrary, it must be developed to its full potential as an organ of sensory apprehension of the universe and also as an instrument of self-expression and effective communication with fellow beings.

In the same way, sex has its proper place and function in the scheme of personality growth. It is an essential factor in independent thinking and living and in the process of individuation. On the one hand, suppression of sex leads to the sapping of vital energies and to loss of creativity. On the other hand, over-indulgence of sex or sexual promiscuity leads to the dissipation of psychic energy. It hinders the channeling of psychic energy toward the fulfillment of higher values. So, the important thing is neither ascetic suppression nor sexual obsession, but transformation of the sexual libido. When sex is accepted as one of the natural functions of life and as a means of expression of genuine love, the dynamics of inner growth projects in due time higher cultural, spiritual and humanistic values beyond sex. Gradually the sexual libido is transformed into the creativity of the self on higher levels and into the pure flame of universal love.

In the same way, the ego has its proper place and function in the scheme of self-development. The ego as the I-consciousness is vital to the growth of individuality. A person whose ego is shattered suffers from loss of self-confidence and self-esteem. He may be reduced to a vegetable. On the other hand, when the ego gets too much inflated, a person becomes conceited, haughty and vainglorious. He makes a nuisance of himself to other people. He inflicts damage on his own self-development, which essentially consists in the transition from vanity to humility, from the egocentric to the cosmocentric outlook. So, in authentic self development, the ego should neither be destroyed nor deified. It must be transformed into the illuminated I-consciousness which the real self is. When illuminated, the I functions as an active center of consciousness of the intrinsic values of life.

Aurobindo speaks of the threefold transformation of our total being: psychic, spiritual and supramental. Without going into any detailed discussion of the metaphysical concepts involved, I should like to express briefly in psychological terms the meaning of his theory.

The first great breakthrough in self-actualization is the awakening of the true spirit of love, of egoless and unmotivated love. It is a radical leap beyond the egocentric outlook. It implies genuine concern for the welfare of others. Perception of Being as the unitary source of all living beings gives rise to the spontaneous feeling of love for all. When a person's whole being is suffused with such spontaneous love, he achieves what Aurobindo calls psychic transformation—transformation of being by the power of love, devotion, and utter dedication to Being.

The next stage in self-transformation is the realization of full freedom and peace—freedom from all emotional bonds of attachment and fixation and the resulting sense of self-sufficiency of self-existence by virtue of union with Being. The sense of freedom and peace flows from the awareness of pure transcendence. Emotions and ecstasies are transformed into a vast feeling of serenity. Ideas and thoughts are transformed into transcendental awareness of Being. Aurobindo has called it spiritual transformation. We may designate it as the transformation of personality by the light of wisdom and the power of freedom.

The final phase of transformation emphasized in integral psychology consists in the transformation of our total being including the physical, the instinctual, the intellectual, and the socio-moral by the light and power of the comprehensive awareness of Being in its fullness. This perfectly prepares one for illumined participation in the creative adventure of life in consonance with the evolutionary urge of Being. Aurobindo has called it supramental transformation. It is the integral transformation of our total being.

Integral Experientialism

The methodology of integral psychology can best be described as integral experientialism. It may also be called total empricism. It broadens the scope of empiricism, sharpens critical analysis, and combines objective investigation with personal integration.

The traditional empirical approach in the West is more

often than not understood in a very narrow sense. In natural sciences it is limited to the data of sense perception such as colors and visible forms, sounds and smell, tactile and gustatory sensibilia. In modern depth psychology the facts of introspective self-awareness as reported by patients as well as mental processes uncovered from the patients' unconscious mind, are included in the scope of empiricism.

In recent times, mystical and transpersonal experiences, various modes of apprehension of transcendence, are attracting the attention of psychologists. William James opened a new vista of thought and broadened the scope of empiricism in his *Varieties of Religious Experience*.[6] Today it is being increasingly realized that in order to obtain a total view of the human psyche, what Maslow calls "peak experiences" of healthy, self-actualizing people should be taken into account no less than the abyss experiences of the mentally ill. Experiences gained by meditative ego-transcendence are no less valuable than the facts of experience disclosed through the psychoanalysis of pathological cases in casting light upon the structure of human reality.

Integral experientialism is therefore a blueprint for thorough investigation of all forms and phases of human experience. It includes in its scope dream experiences as well as waking experiences, drug-induced hallucinatory experiences as well as meditatively acquired ontological insights, dreamless sleep experience as well as transcendental experiences.

Need for Personal Integration

It is not possible for one to understand the meaning and truth-value of transcendental experiences unless he has some personal realization of his own. So it is important for an investigator of integral psychology to undergo the discipline of personal integration resulting in direct awareness of the transpersonal. It is in the light of such personal self-realization that he can comprehend fully the significance of peak experiences of the ontological order.

In investigating the experiences of other people, an integrated psychologist would cease to have an aloof impersonal attitude of cold intellectual analysis. Instead, he would be able to establish a warm, emotional rapport with all subjects, whether self-alienated or self-actualizing. Such a rapport is indeed the essential core of fruitful dialogue. Through an exchange of experiences, through the kind of whole-hearted communication that fully engages two or more concerned individuals, deeper flashes of truth are struck out, increasingly expanding mental horizons. Major emphasis has been given to the fact that it is only by following the inner light of one's own self that the human psyche can be comprehended in its fullness. Personal self-realization, immediate awareness of the inmost core of one's own personality through total psycho-physical discipline, is the *sine qua non* of adequate psychological understanding.

Critical Analysis

Integral psychology recognizes the fact that all knowledge is, as Immanuel Kant says, interpretation of experience. Thought without experience is empty; experience without thought or rational interpretation is blind.

Usually psychologists keep away from philosophical analysis. But man being essentially a thinking animal, the empirical investigation of psychology can hardly be separated from the psychologist's own ground conceptions and tacit metaphysical assumptions. So, when in the name of empiricism a psychologist ignores this fact, he becomes the victim of his unconscious and uncritical assumptions and postulates.

In other words, psychology as the science of the human psyche can hardly be separated completely from philosophy as critical and reflective thinking. Philosophic thinking is an essential function of the human psyche. It is the criticism of all categories, the transcendental analysis of the fundamental assumptions and postulates of all sciences. Integral psychology emphasizes the need for philosophical clarification of its own assumptions and of the assumptions of other schools of psychology.

All psychological investigation should be guided by the integral view of the human psyche. The psyche is the indivisible unity of the physical, the mental and the transpersonal. There is no doubt some qualitative distinction between instinct and intellect, between passion and reason, because there is a touch of the mechanical and the irrational to our instinctual nature. Likewise, there is some qualitative distinction between rational thinking and intuitive apprehension or transpersonal awareness of the ultimate ground of our own existence. But such qualitative distinctions have only an intra-psychic significance. They do not imply the juxtaposition of separate metaphysical principles like matter and mind (Descartes) or energy and spirit (Patanjali). Nor do they imply that the selfless love of man for man or the self-transcending spirit of dedication to Being are only sublimations of the frustrated ego drive. Nor do they imply that only the intuitively apprehended eternal Self is real, so that the body-mind is only an unreal superimposition thereupon.

Conclusion

The foregoing is a brief outline of the orientation, scope, and methology of integral psychology as derived from the basic psychological insights of Sri Aurobindo. It is the hope of the writer that investigators more competent than himself will come forward to carry the germinal ideas set forth herein to further development, more ample ramification, and wider application. With its emphasis upon the need for investigating and analyzing the totality of human experience, integral psychology may play a vital role in the integration of human knowledge—in harmonizing science, religion, art, morality, and mysticism, etc. In exploring the various dimensions of the human psyche, it is guided by the total view of man as an integral part of the cosmic whole.

B. INDIVIDUALITY - RELATEDNESS - TRANSCENDENCE

We have so often a tendency to approach a problem or to contemplate reality in a fragmentary way, analyzing it into parts and trying to synthesize. In that way we become very one-sided in our understanding of the nature of reality. Even though there are different parts in the universe, different constituent elements of reality, every element derives its meaning from the context of the whole in which it exists and functions. Without an awareness of the cosmic whole, we do not fully appreciate and understand the significance of any part.

It is important to have a comprehensive, holistic, integrated view of humanity. The integral view of man implies that no individual is a separate self-existent entity. Just as the different elements of our nature—body, mind, spirit—are interrelated aspects, in the same way, every individual is a factor in a social continuum. We are closely interlinked in our lives and destiny. Individuality conceived as a self-existent atom is an abstraction of our mind; it does not exist. Nobody lives by himself. Human beings become more and more human through social interrelations, interactions.

Broadly speaking, there are three inseparable aspects of human personality: uniqueness or individuality, universality or relatedness, and transcendence. In different schools of philosophy we find that there has been a tendency to over-emphasize one aspect or another. It has not occurred to many people that all these are very essential and interrelated aspects of our being. It is not good to over-emphasize any one of these at the expense of others.

Uniqueness implies that every human individual has an unrepeatable uniqueness of his own. If this is so, then blind conformity to an external standard can never be good for him. If anybody is persuaded to follow a path of unthinking conformity to an external standard, more and more the flame of individuality within him is snuffed out. We can learn from everybody, all persons, in so many different ways, but eventually we have to follow the light of our own self. No matter from what sources we draw elements of truth and value, ultimately it depends upon our ability to assimilate this into the evolving texture of our own being. Ultimately, it is a question of the evolution and fulfillment of our own inner self, which has a unique rhythm of development. As it is said, every human soul is like a delicate flower. It has to bud and blossom, growing from the roots of its own being, even though in the process it assimilates nourishment from different sources.

Individuality is in danger in the present age. On the one hand, we have all become very conscious of our individuality. On the other hand, this very individuality is in great danger of being swallowed up. Everywhere we look there is an attack on our individuality by big corporations, big powers, and even in the universities we are reduced to a number like in a prison.

This injects into our minds a feeling of nothingness. It was in protest of this that the existentialist movement arose.

Out of the East there has developed the integral approach where individuality is recognized as one of the highest goals of life. In traditional mysticism, when you encounter higher consciousness, it has been viewed as the destruction of your individuality. In the integral view, what gets destroyed is your egocentric individuality. But death leads to rebirth. It is your egocentric individuality which is liquidated upon authentic illumination. Out of the ashes of your ignorant individuality is reborn your true illumined self. In order to enter into the light of cosmocentric individuality, the ego has to die. Out of the dissolution of the false identity of the limited egocentric individuality is born the true self, which is imperishable.

Now let us turn to another aspect, interrelatedness. Many people have thought that self-realization requires permanent solitude. Every individual is an integral part of the social organism, however, and in cutting oneself off from the collectivity one denies his position as a member of the human family. It is through social interaction that we can develop this very important aspect of our being.

This idea has been developed by the school of philosophy known as ethical idealism. For example, Albert Schweitzer has developed this view. In the same way, Mahatma Gandhi brought this out. I remember that some newspaper correspondents who came to have an interview with him asked him why as a religious man he did not give much time to prayer and meditation. Gandhi replied that he perceived the presence of God in fellow beings. How could there be any greater form of meditation except in doing service for the good of man? That was his answer.

Just as individuality can be carried to an extreme and one can live a kind of insular existence, similarly universality can also be carried to an extreme. Man has a great knack of carrying things to an extreme and turning truth into falsehood. So, universality can be carried to an extreme when we overemphasize the collective life to the neglect of the creative freedom of individuals.

Another important aspect of our life is, as I said, transcendence. Man is essentially a spiritual being with a spark of freedom within him. Freedom is the self-transcending spirit in man. That is to say, freedom refuses to be bound to any given situation or any given structure. This self-transcending impulse of freedom finds its highest expression when one realizes that he does not have to conform to any external standards and rules. As a spiritual being he has the right to rise above these and find the ground of existence by his own effort. Organized structures may claim that you have to go through them in order to achieve salvation. The essential significance of transcendence is that man in his inmost being is a child of immortality, an imperishable spark of the infinite. As a mode of manifestation of Being, his ultimate goal is union with that ground of existence, transcending all other limitations . . . limitations of a party, a group, this or that particular society or community.

But again, we have carried transcendence to an extreme. Certainly transcendence is a very important part of the human potential, but it is not to be understood in separation from the other factors I have mentioned. It is to be understood in union with society and individuality. That is the essence of the integral view.

So far as one's spiritual aspiration is concerned, there is no doubt that the highest goal is union with Being. When this union is mature, then the individual will be sure to recognize that Being does not exist apart from the world, as the whole world is a manifestation of it. Therefore, it follows that transcendental realization is of prime importance. Then, it must be realized that Being is present in history, in evolution, in social progress. When one realizes this, his reaction is to express the joy and love and light of this understanding in human relations, in social actions, into the fabric of human relations. In that way transcendence, individuality, and universality are harmonized. That contributes to the full flowering of the human potential.

EDUCATION

There is a growing realization that human personality is a multifaceted and multidimensional phenomenon. No scheme of education can therefore be worth its name without a well-rounded program for balanced personality growth of the human individual.

The ideal teacher is one who does not dictate to you, but who helps you to realize your own potential.

A. *EDUCATION OF THE WHOLE MAN*

Mankind can no longer be divided into exclusive segments so that the fortune of one will not affect the fortune of the other. We live in a world of shrinking dimensions with people of different cultural, religious and racial backgrounds coming together. As it is commonly phrased, either we swim together or we sink together. This is the kind of situation in which we exist. Therefore, all those who think about our present-day situation are convinced that global peace is not a pious wish; rather it is a vital necessity for the survival of the human race.

Everybody feels the need for peace. Every great leader talks about it and proclaims its vital importance. However, we find that even though on the intellectual level we are convinced about it, by talking about it and making pledges, in our actual behavior patterns, our day to day dealing with fellow beings, we seem to act paradoxically, showing a yawning chasm, an unbridgeable gulf, between our profession and practice. What is the reason, and what can be done about it? This is the crux of the whole crisis that confronts us today.

It is with regard to this matter that many people feel education plays a vital role—not only in our ways of thinking, in our outlook on life, and in our sense of values, but also in our actual behavior. When we think about the role of education in human life, in our conduct and in our relations with one another, we immediately feel that there is a great need today for an overhaul of the entire educational system. Most probably it is a kind of vague, intuitive feeling of this vital need which is at the root of widespread turmoil and disturbances in the university and college campuses throughout the world.

I should like to say a word in this connection about what is called integral education—education of the whole man. Different educational leaders are thinking along these lines. Some express it in slightly different ways, but this is one question which seems to be in the thoughts of the foremost leaders of the world, i.e., "how can we change our educational system in order to emphasize the concept of education of the whole man?"

The educational system, as it operates today, does not take into account the whole man, nor does it take into account the whole world. It is concerned neither with global consciousness nor the integral man in his full integrity and in the multidimensional richness of his total existence. We find that these concepts do not go into the educational planning. These are certainly not the concepts which determine the educational policy of the different institutions today. Unless we go to the root of the problem and find out what are the fundamental ideas which are responsible for the educational structure as we see it today, and make changes there, the most desirable changes in human life cannot be brought about. This is the meaning of integral education—education which is based upon the concept of the total man and education which is based upon the total human situation, the global situation.

A father one day called his son to his side and said, "Son, you have the habit of seeing things double, seeing everything as two." Energetically protesting the son said, "No! If I really saw things double, then I would see four moons." He was in the habit of seeing the moon as two, and so he said, "If I saw things double, then I would see four moons instead of two." Think about the import of this. Simply for the father to say, "You are mistaken, you have double vision" is not going to help the son, as we see in this illustration.

This is like much of our education. We just point out mistakes and say this is wrong and that is right, and nobody believes it. Even by reading books and committing them to memory, we can express these things again to other people, but they don't necessarily believe them. Oh, we may believe ideas as something written in the book, or something said by a professor, and be in a position to repeat these things parrot-like and feel good about it—but not believe, to the extent that the truth becomes a dynamic force in our actual life, a dynamic force in our behavior patterns. Our concern is how to drive a force in our actual life, a dynamic force in our behavior patterns. Our concern is how to drive a force into the depths of one's soul so that it becomes not only a set of words, or a system of propositions, but a vital force in our course of living.

What can be done? Well, what can be done about the boy who sees double? Let us go back to that and perhaps we shall find an answer right there. We have seen that for somebody to point out that he is seeing double is not going to do him any good because he would not believe them. The only way to rectify this situation is to make him see that he sees double, otherwise nothing will happen. How can we do that? Well, we can find out the cause, *if* we go to the root cause of the matter, perhaps we may find something is wrong with his visual organ. All that may be necessary is a simple operation to remove this deficiency and correct his power of vision. Then nobody will have to tell him that he is seeing double because he will simply see single. It sounds very simple, but this is the essence of the whole matter.

You see, at present, we are all in the habit of seeing things double. This is due to some defect in our present level of consciousness. We are all seeing things double without knowing it. We look at the world, and we suffer from the incurable habit of slicing the world into pieces, dividing it into antagonistic camps depending upon whatever the ideological or philosophical or religious background of an individual may be. Carl Jung has brought it out very nicely in his *The Undiscovered Self!* Further, R. D. Laing portrays this in *The Divided Self.*[2] When the self is divided into two, the world is divided into two. When we look at the world, we often divide it into two antagonistic groups, one is very good and the other is very bad—an extension into the world of our inner division, dividing our fellow beings into good guys and bad guys, or seeing things double.

Looking within yourself, you will find that there is a double personality there. There is an empirical self and there is what is called a transcendental self. There is a phenomenal self and there is a spiritual self. Once in a while we seem to be in touch with our spiritual self, and then we catch a glimpse of the reality of such values as peace, freedom, justice and love. We just catch a glimpse of these things. But as soon as it comes to our activities, we are plunged into our empirical self, we get enmeshed in the network of ideas, feelings and desires of what is called the empirical self—the phenomenal self—which has an absolutely different rhythm and law of operation altogether. In this self all those beautiful ideas completely vanish. On that level we find that all these beautiful ideas and visions of lofty values completely disappear, they appear like shadows when it comes to the actual activities of our life operations from day to day. So right within ourself there is this split personality, this divided self.

In spite of this division and the deeper problems that go along with this division, we somehow manage to adjust to our environment and get along but still, even though there is this normalcy because of some adjustment that we make, that does not mean that there is not suffering inside. All of us so-called normal human beings suffer from a good deal of anguish or agony of the soul, all kinds of mental, psychological, spiritual problems. We intuitively feel that these problems are there inwardly hindering our personality growth, our self-development, obstructing our urge for self-perfection and continuous unfoldment of the inner potentialities of our being. Deep down in our heart we feel that, and therefore we suffer from the existential anxiety which is present in all human beings, however normal we appear to be.

Our educational institutions ordinarily do not address this problem. The emphasis normally is gathering information about a lot of things. But accumulation of information, however indefinitely it may go on, will not bring about that inner cure, will not eliminate the habit of seeing things double, which is an internal thing. The kind of operation which is necessary in order to help us out of our dualistic thinking is a nondual experience. Then we begin to see things one again. The world is one, and all human beings, regardless of differences of race, religion, culture, and ideology, are members of one international human family. Until and unless we have this inner vision, not as just an intellectual idea which doesn't change behavior, but as an inner vision, spiritual experience, or emotional experience, of this fundamental unity of existence and inseparable interdependence of all individual human beings and races and peoples of the world, then we are not going to set aside the habit of dualistic thinking. For this, what is necessary is the discipline which brings about an inner growth of consciousness. This is a matter of vital importance—this inner change of consciousness.

As Aldous Huxley[3] says, there is one perennial, universal philosophy, but we are so much under the spell of dualistic and pluralistic thinking, that even though there is really one universal truth and one universal perennial philosophy, we have the habit of creating many philosophies, many philosophical systems. And we not only see the many, but also we think that they are mutually exclusive of one another.

Often an individual thinks that his way of philosophical thinking is absolutely right and others are wrong. We are living in the same world and there is one ultimate reality, but depending upon our point of view, our angle of vision, depending upon the circumstances of our life, we perceive that one ultimate truth in so many diverse forms. Each form of expression of that ultimate reality has some relative validity. We can know that only when we are in a position somehow to see the universe as a whole, in its entirety. Intellectually, the difference seems very easy to understand and also very simple, but when it comes to the question of our dealings with one another and our dealings in this world, it means the difference between life and death. It means the difference between death or destruction on the one hand, and creation and construction on the other.

The difference between dualistic or pluralistic thinking which is characteristic of the conceptual level of consciousness on which we operate usually in our life must be distinguished from the nondualistic level of consciousness, which is a profound potential of man. This ability to see things from the standpoint of an integral consciousness is present in each one of us. That is the true meaning of the latent divinity in man. When the great seers tell us that God is present in us, in all human beings, without exception, this is the true meaning of it—that we have this profound spiritual potential; potential for rising from the level of dualistic consciousness to the level of nondual experience of the universe as a whole. This is the profoundest potential of man. And only when we shall experience this transition from the dualistic or pluralistic thinking to the nondualistic way of seeing everything, can the ideal human society or the global society be founded.

This is not just wishful thinking. According to some of the greatest thinkers of the world, this is the fundamental drift of human evolution. We are involved in the process of planetary evolution, which is leading in that direction, in the direction of eventually lifting man from his present dualistic level up to the nondualistic, unitive level of consciousness. In order to translate this dream into reality, this radical change in human consciousness is of paramount importance.

As we study the history of man's cultural and spiritual growth, we find that there are some shining examples of the realization of this potential through the great spiritual masters of the world, like Jesus Christ, or Buddha, or Lao-tse, or Moses, or Krishna. But today, it should not be difficult for us to understand that they were all human beings like us, not anybody descending upon this planet from out of the blue. They were all human beings, and it just so happened that in the course of evolution these profound spiritual potentials were realized in their lives. This divine potentiality is present in all of us. The kind of nondual vision of the truth, which seemed to be the prerogative of a few, gradually is going to become a common possession.

Until and unless the educational system incorporates into its curriculum certain disciplines which can help in bringing about this inner change of consciousness, then it is not nourishing the desire for self-perfection which is in every being. In modern psychology this is called the growth impulse; every human being has a growth impulse. And the ultimate goal of this impulse is the transition from the dualistic, conceptual way of thinking to a nondualistic, transconceptual level of consciousness. Since this is a potential of every human being, all of us can do something about it to bring about this radical change of consciousness.

This is where the need for spiritual discipline enters. This spiritual discipline, which is a very general word, includes three kinds of essential disciplines. One is psychophysical discipline; another is training in values; and the third is ontological discipline.

Most educational systems carry no provisions for value consciousness. Previously, there was training in value consciousness in the form of ethics and religion, but nowadays education has been separated from religion because of the fact that old religious ideas have become outdated and we have not yet found positive spiritual substitutes for this whole religious idea. As a result, schools, colleges, universities are without any training in the development of value consciousness.

What I call ontological discipline helps us towards actualizing the spiritual potential, the potential of integral consciousness, which is in all human beings. This is direct experiential knowledge of fundamental truths of existence. It implies a sensitivity to profound cognitions of Being.

A balanced educational process would include cultivation of value consciousness and Being-cognition as well as enhancing the physical and intellectual disciplines which now exist. The integral completeness of man must be brought to awareness in education if we are to aid in developing the potentials present within.

B. *INTERNATIONAL COMMUNITY EDUCATION*

International community education is certainly an idea whose time has come. Its idea has come because it is the most fitting response to the challenge of our times. It is an idea which is doubly ripe, first as an age-long dream of human aspiration and second, as a basic need of planetary evolution. The idea is sure to catch fire, evoke enthusiasm wherever people are ready, and thus play a vital role in laying the foundation for the devoutly-wished human unity and global peace.

Education is indeed the most effective agency by which genuine change of human consciousness and enduring transformation of human behavior can be accomplished. Global education alone can build a solid structure of global peace and progress which has been a dream of poets for a long time, a vision of prophets, and a utopia of scientists.

We are all conscious today of our existence on a small planet of ever shrinking dimensions. The breathtaking speed of our jet age makes it look like a global village. Under these circumstances it is sadly self-defeating to allow cultural and ideological differences to stubbornly continue as a stumbling block to human unity and cooperation toward fulfilling the human dream of a kingdom of heaven on earth.

The concept of worldwide community education requires for its successful implementation a multi-disciplinary approach on the one hand and humanistically oriented mobilization of mass energy on the other.

Outlined below are a few most fundamental principles of integral or holistic education for the world community aimed at the building of one internationally unified global society:

1. Promotion of intercultural, interracial, and interreligious understanding.
2. Acceptance of ideological diversity within the global unity of humankind.
3. Affirmation of the intrinsic dignity of all individuals, men and women, everywhere in the world.
4. The essential equality of all races, and peoples and nations of the world.
5. Interdisciplinary coordination and synthesis.
6. Education for the whole person in his/her multi-dimensional richness.
7. Comparative studies East and West.
8. Physical fitness and sports.
9. Developmental alternatives to drug use, social disorientation, and counterculture protest.
10. Semantic clarification for effective communication.
11. Opportunity for esthetic refinement and creative self-expression.
12. Teachers' training in divergent conceptual frameworks for the same universal truth.

METHODOLOGY

Integral thinking is based on the principle of unity in diversity. It is only when we discover this principle that real harmony can be established in oneself and in human relations.

We see that if a person becomes overspecialized, then he loses his human value, his spirit of human value. He becomes very mechanized in his attitude. Without a wholistic, synoptic vision of reality, one cannot be creative. The secret of creativity is to have a wholistic vision of reality.

A. *THE INTEGRAL METHOD*

The more we understand the essential structure of the universe as a whole, the more we gain insight into the essential structure of man. The obverse must also be true. The more we understand the essential structure of man, the more we gain insight into the unfathomable mystery of Being.

The integral method is derived from this ontological insight which sees man, as Being, as the dynamic unity of all opposites. The path leading to this insight may be described as integral thinking. The integral world view and integral thinking are in truth two sides of the same coin. They are mutually dependent and jointly relevant for man's search for total truth. The method of integral thinking represents a dynamic integration of the scientific, phenomenological and dialectical methods of the West and the self-analytical, psycho-integrative, nondual value disciplines of the East.

Integral thinking recognizes that one uniform methodology cannot be blindly applied to all areas of human experience and to all disciplines of knowledge. Every discipline has its own unique features because every special area of experience has distinctive characteristics of its own. It reasonably follows that the methodology adopted in a special field of inquiry must closely follow the essential structure and specific goal of that field.

For instance, in natural sciences like physics and chemistry, the concept of mechanistic determination and the principle of physical measurements are without a doubt quite appropriate and fruitful. In investigating biological phenomena, however, the category of purposiveness and holistic function is indispensable. The response pattern of a particular organ of a living being cannot be understood without reference to other interrelated organs and their collective subordination to the overall purpose of the organism as a whole. For all practical purposes life is a qualitatively different category of existence than matter.

Similarly, in the study of psychology, the behavior pattern of a human being can hardly be fully understood without reference to the conscious and unconscious motivational dynamics of man acting as an individual or a group. Outwardly similar behavior bears surprisingly different meanings when viewed in the light of different motivations. For instance, a person may kill another fellow being either on suspicion of violent enmity, or in self-defense against actual attack, or out of righteous indignation against his anti-social life style, or under the irresistable urge of an irrational urge to kill, or with a pious desire to liquidate those who obstruct the kingdom of heaven. We see that to understand the mind, we need the assitance of values different from physics and biology.

When we come to such value disciplines as logic, esthetics, ethics, and spiritual self-disciplines, the method of quantitative measurement or physical reductionism can hardly be of much help. Value is an essentially different category or dimension of Being bound to elude the grasp of all quantitative measurement. How can you appreciate the meaning of a poem by analyzing the grammatical structure of the language in which it is couched? How can you fathom the significance of the idea of the Good by analyzing the pattern of one's organic responses to environmental changes? How can you glimpse the glory of love and joyful self-giving by measuring the heart beat and the pulse rate? How can you comprehend the transcendent value of a man's cosmic vision of truth by measuring the alpha wave pattern of his brain?

All such measurements can have some limited usefulness only when you have found a way, a qualitatively different way, to appreciate the transpersonal value experiences of humans. True it is that suitable changes in the quantitative configurations of the actual world mysteriously give rise to new values as emergent qualities. But such emergent qualities or transcendent values can hardly be reduced to and understood in terms of quantitative measurements.

For the purpose of active realization of authentic human values, it is of paramount importance that a person must have a first-hand moving experience of higher values. It is in the absence of personal value experiences of an inspiring nature that people lend themselves to exploitative manipulation, whether commercial, or political or religious. Failure to distinguish between quantity and quality, between fact and ideal value, is a basic ingredient of the crisis of our civilization today.

All disciplines of human knowledge are in essence organized systems of ideas or verbal propositions. They represent abstractions of thought from the concrete fullness of the real, designed to fulfill some definite goal or purpose of life—whether intellectual, ethical, religious or political.

Since a thought system is then essentially a map, to be distinguished from the territory of the real, it is unthinking confusion to equate it with reality itself. Since a map is not a territory but a sketchy guidechart indicating possible lines of movement and action in the real world, no ideological scheme, whether theological or metaphysical, or scientific or political can be said to exhaust the multidimensional fullness of the universe. It should be clearly recognized that the universe, essentially different from all conceptual maps, necessarily transcends all philosophical, religious, scientific and political ideologies. The universe is the ground and the comprehensive unity of all thought systems without itself being a determinant system.

This gives rise to a non-dogmatic and non-doctrinaire attitude, to a genuine respect for opposite viewpoints and to a synoptic vision of the universe in its integral fullness. When we clearly grasp the epistemological relativity and pragmatic limitation of all conceptual systems forming the components of human knowledge, the attitude of cocksure arrogance or doctrinaire complacency is disclosed as a mark of ignorance. No theologian or metaphysician, no mystic or scientist has a reasonable right to think that he has all the answers or the cream of all knowledge in his hands.

Since no definite viewpoint can exhaust the fullness of the infinity of Being, wisdom dictates an attitude of humility and sincere receptivity to the light of truth shining through other viewpoints. A closed mind is the worse enemy of balanced growth. There is perpetual need for free and frank exchange of ideas and experiences with fellow beings in our cooperative adventure in search of the ultimate. Man is essentially an unfinished business. His life is unceasing search for truth and increasing manifestation of the infinite glory thereof in life and society.

A genuine respect for opposite viewpoints is much more than just the spirit of tolerance. A person who feels cocksure about his complete possession of the absolute truth has no urge to compare notes. He may at best tolerate other views out of pity or politeness or paternal helpfulness. He is in no mood to listen to others, and to understand different perspectives. His humility is a social pose, a "holy affectation". He needs mature understanding to perceive the limitation of one's even encyclopedic knowledge. Without awareness of the finitude of human knowledge it is not really possible to open one's mind beyond the prison walls of the ego in a spirit of genuine receptivity to the multitudinous expression of the one truth. True respect for others is born of the vision of truth in others. Active participation in authentic dialogue is impossible without a glimpse of the inexhaustible mystery of Being.

Dichotomous thinking is a logical sequel to the mind's dogmatic attitude. When a person dogmatically believes that his chosen aspect of reality is the absolute truth, the excluded aspect naturally appears false to him. When, for instance, the supernatural realm is believed to be absolutely true and good, the natural order appears false and evil to him. On the other hand, when a person pins his faith in the natural order of existence, as the ultimate reality, the supernatural obviously appears an illusion. If a person dogmatically believes that his own worldview or political ideology is the ultimate truth or the supreme good for all mankind, then the opposite world view or political ideology will naturally be perceived as the devil's trap.

The ideological dichotomy produces subjective polarization. If a particular creed or ideology is the supreme good, it has a sovereign claim to our total allegiance. Nothing but unflinching devotion and unreserved surrender is the right response to the ultimate good. A god is—by his very nature—uncompromisingly jealous. He brooks no rivalry in winning the human soul. Total commitment to the unconditional good also involves total rejection and ruthless destruction of the challenging opponent. From the dogmatic's standpoint, the challenger is not only no good, he is absolute evil. So he becomes the target of the concentrated fury of destructive impulse.

The same psychological truth about the polarization of behavior may also be expressed in another way. When we focus our love and devotion on one thing—one particular creed, country or conceptual system—as the only ultimate reality, our psychic energy becomes sharply polarized. Attachment and advocacy are bestowed upon the beloved object, the chosen deity. The impulses of hostility and disgust are forcefully directed against any opposition, the menacing evil. Thus a love/hate syndrome develops within the psyche. It corresponds to the God/devil dichotomy in the outside world.

However, as soon as it is realized that no special component of the universe, nor any specific conceptual system, can possibly represent the ultimate or absolute truth, the dichotomies of thought get dissolved. That clears the ground for the growth of a balanced attitude. One begins to see things as they truly are. The distinctions made by disciplined thought are found to represent relatively valid value-distinctions. They don't represent polar distinctions between absolute good and absolute evil; nor do they represent divisions in existence, separate and discontinuous realities. Neither do they imply an unreal opposition between reality and illusion.

The conceptual understanding, a pragmatic function of the mind, makes the aforesaid distinctions serve the practical purposes of life. But the intellect then loses sight of the pragmatic orientation of the mind and misconstrues these distinctions into separate and discontinuous realities, or into mutually antagonistic principles of value and disvalue. It thus commits the fallacy of substantializing abstractions or the fallacy of misplaced concreteness.

Integral or nondichotomous thinking rejects both the metaphysical as well as the theological interpretation of dichotomies of thought in absolutistic terms. Dualities are neither sharp divisions in reality nor irreconcilable opposites of value and disvalue. They are in essence complimentary half truths clamoring for reconciliation in unifying categories of comprehensive thinking.

*   *   *   *   *   *

What is meant by the doctrine of the Identity of Opposites? This was developed in the Eastern tradition very elaborately. In this country, in recent times, many psychologists especially have been fascinated with this idea on account of their advancing knowledge of the human psyche. In the functioning of the psyche this law of opposites is very much in evidence.

I say that we always understand a particular idea or theory or truth best when we contrast it with its opposite. This is why comparative study is very stimulating—it makes our ideas sharp, bringing basic concepts into focus, resulting in greater understanding.

The doctrine of Identity of Opposites is in direct contrast with the Law of Excluded Middle, of Aristotle, which says that opposites or contradictions exhaust the whole universe of discourse, the whole range of possibility, that there is no middle path. This means that there is no middle ground between contradictories. This has been very prevalent in Western culture, giving rise to all kinds of dichotomies. Whereas in Eastern culture, which has been predominately mystical and spiritual, it is just the opposite—the doctrine of the middle path has been emphasized. The discovery of that middle is the secret of synthesizing opposites. Everywhere in actual life we find that opposites meet, and there is always a middle ground which it is our task to discover, because that gives us the secret of balanced growth or integrated self-development. Also, this is the secret to attaining an integral vision of the total truth.

*   *   *   *   *   *

There are some universal truths which from the standpoint of every discipline of knowledge can be conceptualized, can be expressed in terms of that particular discipline. The same truth can be translated into every discipline of knowledge . . . mathematics, psychology, cosmology, ontology, or philosophy. Truth is truth. And if we understand the essential structure of truth, it is fascinating to see how it can be translated into the language of every discipline of knowledge. This is why there is an increasing emphasis these days upon interdisciplinary studies.

Our knowledge and civilization began with the unity of all disciplines, simple primitive unity of all the branches of knowledge, and that was Philosophy. Philosophy was the mother of all sciences.

Gradually, as we began to pay attention to more details, it became necessary for different sciences to branch out. For the sake of detailed and thorough investigation, it became necessary to have the separate disciplines. But we are realizing today that if we separate these too much, that certainly creates a problem. After all, life is one, the universe is one, and if you keep all the branches of knowledge separate, then you miss the vital truth, the living truth of life. So, in order to understand and practice the living truth of life, you have to do some interdisciplinary study; you have to understand how truths of one science are related to truths of another science. If you don't have that, then you become fragmented in outlook. We are now, therefore, moving toward a more sophisticated unity. We started with primitive, naive unity, and then that unity was pulverized into the multiplicity of sciences and branches of knowledge. Now again we are feeling the need for harmonizing all the fragments of knowledge into a comprehensive synthesis, which would be a very sophisticated kind of unity.

Too much partitioning and fragmentation makes us lose sight of goals and values. It deprives us of the unitary vision of truth and the sense of value, because value is a gestalt property. Value is the property of the configuration of all things. So, if you indulge in too much separation and fragmentation, then you lose sight of the ultimate meaning of life, then we are left with a dead corpse of knowledge, mechanized knowledge, and not real wisdom. Wisdom degenerates into technical, informative knowledge—lots of information, but the light has gone out; the spirit of love and compassion has gone out of it; the sense of direction is lost. In order to restore this vision of truth and the appreciation of higher values, we have to bring together all the separated branches of knowledge.

* * * * * *

With regard to an important philosophical truth, you must remember that you will not be able to grasp it fully at one time. So, it would be better to be patient. First of all, just hear it and listen to it, and then later on you have to think about it, you have to meditate on it. This is the procedure in our philosophical development. Never expect that as soon as you hear something you will fully understand it. After hearing it, your attempt will be just to understand it in whatever measure that you can. And then you have to have patience and self-confidence; self-confidence in the sense of your belief, your faith that the more you think about it, the more you meditate on it, the more the inner significance will come out for you. This is the whole purpose of reflection, contemplation, meditation. Try to look at it from different standpoints, different aspects. Thrash it out in your mind. Then after you have done your thinking, even that is not enough in order to grasp the full significance of it. You have to go beyond even the thinking level. You have to meditate. As you meditate on it, the idea which was more or less clearly understood on the mental level becomes transformed into a living, flaming experience of the truth, a direct vision of the truth. That is when you have full conviction. Before that you can rest assured that there will always be some doubt, some imperfection in your understanding. You have to accept that fact. One has to go through these different phases. Then it becomes fully clear, but not only clear, it becomes a dynamic force in your consciousness. It becomes a living thing, not just an idea, not even just an article of faith, but a living truth which is a deep conviction born of your personal experience.

B. *INTEGRAL DIALECTICS*

Integral Dialectics is a methodological postulate of the integral worldview. It is also the most essential technique of integral self-actualization or the full flowering of the human potential.

According to Indian philosophy,[1] the Supreme Being, the One without a second, became many by producing dualities. Herein lies the most hidden secret of all creation and evolution—self-multiplication through polarization of energy. The nondual Being polarizes itself into the fundamental dualities of spirit and nature, mind and matter, God and world, light and darkness, heaven and earth, logos and eros. To use Eastern terminology, the all-encompassing Brahman or Tao or Tai Chi polarizes itself into the dualities of *purusa* and *prakriti*, *siva* and *sakti*, *yang* and *yin*, *hsing* and *ming*, *yab* and *yum*.

What is true of the infinite is likewise true of the infinitesimal; of every little living thing reflecting an image of the infinite. The tiny germ cell, singing the supreme song of creation, divides itself into two cells; the two cells become four cells; and so it goes until the humming of countless life forms begins to fill the whole world.

Whereas this movement of creation is the division of the One into self-multiplying dualities, dialectics is the opposite movement to resolve all kinds of dualities back into the One. It advances from lower to higher organized wholes of polarity, from less inclusive to more inclusive systems of harmonized duality, until the nondual reality of Being is attained. Reality's creative urge consists in the movement of energy from the relatively undifferentiated whole toward a continuously increasing self-differentiating of the whole. The human mind's quest for truth is the movement of consciousness from the dynamic tension between opposites (thesis and antithesis) toward more and more inclusive syntheses embracing the wholeness of Being.

In Western philosophy, Hegel and Marx applied the dialectical method on a grand scale and developed the monumental thought systems of dialectical idealism and dialectical materialism respectively. But on account of their historical limitations imposed by the rationalistic tradition originating in ancient Greece, dialectics remained an incomplete thing in their hands. Even though Marx had the courage to stand Hegel on his head by developing a system with exactly the opposite starting point, he had no better success in shaking loose from the ingrained rationalistic commitment. Due to their fundamental rationalistic assumption—identifying reality with thought—both of them started with an abstraction of thought, concluded with an abstraction of thought, and left the stage of philosophical history with an abstract faith in perfection.

Hegel started with the notion of Being conceived as the most abstract of all universals serving as the highest category of classification. But absolutely featureless Being is indistinguishable from Nonbeing, which is naturally incapable of producing anything.[2] Thus the Hegelian dialectic originates under extremely inauspicious circumstances. Nevertheless, Hegel was a mighty genius. By his extraordinary magic of conceptual jugglery, he produced out of an empty bag the most magnificent philosophy of absolute idealism the world has ever seen. By breathing into emptiness the concentrated current of metaphysical speculation, he presented to the people a "marvelous ballet of bloodless categories". Following the rhythm of this ballet, he brought the whole history of Western philosophy to its crowning fulfillment in his own thought-system which he considered to be the last word of philosophic wisdom.

Marx learned from Hegel the dialectical secret of absolute truth. But having placed Hegel of the pedestal upside down, Marx started with matter and with the materialistic or economic motivation of man. He naturally concluded with the absolute truth of a perfectly classless society as the ultimate goal and the final scene of the drama of history.

It requires no extraordinary insight to find out that universal matter also is an abstraction of thought. It is merely an abstract hypothesis to explain the infinitely variegated events, processes and experiences of life. The economic motivation, considered by itself, is a mere abstraction held in isolation from the intellectual, ethical, mythological, religious, magical, and supernatural motivations with which it is inextricably bound up. The economic arrangement of society conceived in terms of control of the means of production is another abstraction unduly magnified beyond all proportion in respect of its importance as compared with the emotional, ethical, religious and political aspects of society. The chain of reasoning which begins with an abstraction is bound to end up with an abstraction.

Among human individuals there is obviously an unequal distribution of all manner of divergent qualities and talents.

Whereas some seem to develop uncommon leadership qualities, others seem to have a natural disposition to mind their own business and live peacefully under the protection of the strong. Thus, some kind of distinction is bound always to remain. Moreover, there is no reason why class distinction should necessarily be an evil thing, so long as equal growth opportunities are justly provided to all.

In the ultimate analysis it is the human factor which counts most. No matter to what extent the economic and political structure of a society be drastically overhauled, until and unless there is a real transformation of inner consciousness—a genuine change of heart, as Gandhi would say, exploitation and injustice can hardly be eliminated from society. It is not a change of the economic structure or of the political fabric alone, but a multi-front attack on human problems that is imperatively necessary for establishing an ideal human society on earth. Human problems are of a psychological, ethical, and intellectual nature as well as economic and political.

There is another wrong assumption which vitiates the dialectics of Hegel and Marx. In perfecting the dialectical method, is there any need to start with a hypothetical beginning and to conclude with a hypothetical end? Is not time a beginningless and endless process? We are never quite sure exactly what the absolute beginning of creation or evolution was like, nor can we prescribe an absolutely perfect model to the process of global evolution. Nor can we be sure that the perfect consummation of our present trend of social evolution will not be followed by a new model of perfection with a new beginning. Why speculate on the basis of a determinate beginning and determinate end? A glimpse of the immeasurable richness of life reveals the cyclical movement as the most appropriate form in which Time can serve as Being's creative medium of self-expression.

Integral Dialectics focuses on the most fundamental dualities of life and reality—matter and mind, nature and spirit, world and God, the phenomenal and the transcendental, etc. On the subjective side it focuses on such polarities in the human psyche as the extraverted and introverted tendencies, ascending and descending movement of consciousness, search for the self and search for Being, physical hunger for food and spiritual hunger for truth, thirst for love and quest of power, love of life and fascination with death.

The essence of Integral Dialectics consists in reconciling such polarities into the kind of comprehensive unity of which they are seemingly conflicting but really complementary self-expressions. It further consists in harmonizing opposite movements of consciousness into integral visions of truth as the divine outflowering of evolutionary emergence.

In what follows an attempt will be made to illustrate the essential structure of integral dialectics in terms of man's philosophical search for truth as well as his spiritual quest of self-perfection.

Search for Being

The philosophic search for truth always leads us sooner or later towards some kind of encounter with ultimate reality or Being. As we contemplate the mystery of Being, its two apparently opposite characteristics immediately swim into our field of vision. First, Being must be the creative source of the endless variations of nature and the bewildering diversities of life. In other words, it must be creative energy (*Shakti*). Secondly, Being must be eternally perfect, the unchanging background of the ever-changing world, so that it can stand on its own and serve as the ultimate ground of the universe or as the supreme unifying principle of the cosmic manifold.

It is thus immediately evident that contemplation of the nature of ultimate reality discloses two fundamental opposites as its essential structure. A profound mystery instantly challenges our philosophic thinking. How can unchanging existence dwell together with ever-changing creative energy in the heart of the same supreme reality?

Being, as infinite existence, must be void of all determinations, of qualities, functions, attributes, actions, movements. To have any specific determination means to be finite and limited. To engage in any action or movement also implies finitude. To function as the substratum of qualities, essences, attributes, and energies is to betray its character as an intellectual construction—an offspring of the application to Being of the category of substance-quality.

It is the aforesaid logic of category-transcendence which has compelled such Hindu philosophers as Samkara to declare that Being is absolutely indeterminable *(Nirguna)*.[3] The same logic compelled Buddha to announce that the ground or bedrock of all existence is nonbeing, void or emptiness *(Shunyata)*, because Being is also an intellectual category. Buddha, however, conveniently forgot that nonbeing, void or emptiness also is an intellectual category, a verbal and conceptual determination of the indeterminable. Spinoza, in the West, encountered the same problem but decided to stay away from it. From his own psychological standpoint he probably arrived at some kind of solution just by looking in the other direction, but certainly left his followers in a quandary. Some interpreters thought that Spinoza's one infinite reality was absolutely void of all determinations, because "all determination is negation". Others believed that Spinoza's Nature-God was one infinite substance endowed with infinite attributes.[4]

The inevitable sequel to extreme nondualism is the emergence of a new kind of dualism. According to a fundamental law of dialectics, when one member of a polarity is carried to its furthest extreme, it automatically turns into its radical opposite. For instance, indeterminable being turns into nonbeing, and conceptualized nonbeing turns into being, as Hegel brilliantly demonstrated. Likewise, the nondualism of pure being or nonbeing, carried to its furthest extreme, suddenly gets strangely metamorphosed into the absolute dualism of the absolute and the relative, ultimate reality and unreal appearance, eternal perfection and the creative energy of time.

So long as one fails to *integrate* Energy, the dynamic source of the relative world, into the reality of the absolute or the ultimate, one is bound to land upon the dualism of the ultimate and the relative, or the dualism of Being and Energy. It may be said that the Energy which is responsible for the projection of the relative and phenomenal world is nothing but primal ignorance. But upon close examination, this will be found to be a subtle form of self-delusion, or a kind of verbal jugglery void of any value. Primal ignorance also has a right to be explained. From where does it come? Is it real or unreal? How can it function as the creative source of the cosmic manifold with all their processes of life and death and products of comedy and tragedy?

It may be said that the realm of relativity or the phenomenal world, the sphere of primal ignorance, seems to be real only from the empirical standpoint. From the ultimate standpoint of supreme knowledge it is just nothing. But this, again, is only a clever shifting of the focus of the problem, without amounting to any sensible solution at all. The necessity now irrepressibly arises for an honest account of the origin of the empirical standpoint. We are now pushed into the unmitigated dualism of two irreconcilable standpoints, the standpoints of knowledge and ignorance, representing two unbridgeable levels of consciousness. It is this kind of psychological dichotomy which drives people either into pathetic schizophrenia or ascetic self-destruction. The polarization of psychic energy resulting from extreme nondualism produces the euphemism of either holy indifference to the world or of ecstatic self-deification. Such are the terrible consequences of the tyranny of words throughout history.

Logical Abstractionism

In our view, metaphysical problems are traceable, more often than not, to the mind's unconscious tendency to substantialize an abstraction, or to equate an abstracted part with the whole. As a consequence, metaphysicians are frequently inclined to start with logical abstractions such as empty Being or contentless Nothing or structureless Becoming, etc. Since *ex nihilo nihil fit*— from nothing comes nothing—naturally they end up explaining nothing.

Those who try to control this abstractionist tendency make sure to start with reality in the concrete, with absolute immediacy. Extreme empiricism and extreme mysticism vie with each other to accomplish this. But unfortunately, absolute immediacy invariably proves to be an exceedingly elusive thing—some kind of will o' wisp. Man as a thinking animal is destined always to live, move and hunger for knowledge within the limits of the field of his mediating thought.

Karl Marx, determined to have his feet planted on the solid ground of perceptual immediacy, started with universal matter, with the supremacy of the materialistic desire for food and survival, and with the universal will to power on the part of the capitalists. But universal matter is no less an abstraction of thought than universal life, universal mind, universal spirit, and the like. Similarly, the word capitalist is an abstraction of thought. There are always different kinds of capitalists, and there are important concrete differences of quality among them. Similarly the will to power or to exploit is another abstract universal. In the concrete texture of human consciousness it is always to be found inextricably intertwined with the will to live and love, the will to know and realize the Good, the will to help and serve, to give and share, as well as to take and make profits.

Rationalistic dialecticians are unconsciously influenced by the false methodological postulate of abstractionsim or logical atomism. They unreflectingly assume that a sufficiently large number of abstract notions, empty concepts, logical atoms, brought together in a clever combination, will get miraculously metamorphosed into the concrete fullness of reality or into the flesh-and-blood vitality of living evolution. In other words, they are predisposed to think, on the basis of metaphysical faith, that abstract notions are the atoms of absolute truth or undeniable building blocks of ultimate reality. Since this assumption is unconscious, the absurdity of deriving concrete reality from thin abstractions, usually escapes the rationalist's attention. Moreover, intense wishful thinking tends to block embarrassing facts from vision. In consequence, the system-builder becomes deluded into the flattering conviction that he has somehow received from some anonymous higher authority the honor and privilege of reproducing in his own mind the original mystery of creation. Among the human mind's countless methods of self-kidding, this is perhaps the most subtle of all. This must be the most invincible trick of Maya, the principle of original Ignorance and the benign mother of illusions.

Reaffirmation of Wholeness

Integral Dialectics rejects this entire abstractionist way of metaphysical reconstruction of the universe out of conceptual abstractions or bloodless logical atoms. Needless to say, by logical atoms I mean empty abstract notions believed to be reality's ultimate building blocks.

Integral Dialectics starts with the universe as a whole, with reality as concrete multidimensional fullness. It starts with the indivisible totality of human experience, with the whole spectrum of human consciousness, of which sensory experience and intuitive apprehension of the whole are two inseparable poles. It is the integrated unity of human consciousness—the perfect integration of all the levels of experience—which alone reveals the wholeness of reality or Being.

Let us therefore reaffirm the reality of the cosmic whole as both the alpha and the omega of philosophic thinking, as the true beginning and the true end of all spiritual quest and metaphysical speculation. Let us also reaffirm the reality of our human experience-continuum including waking, dream, sleep and *samadhi* as the multi-colored reflection in our human mind of the multi-level Being or cosmic continuum.

As the comprehensive unity of the cosmic manifold, the fullness of reality is called Being, the ultimate ground of all that exists. As the creative source of the cosmic manifold the same reality is perceived as infinite Energy. There is absolutely no justification for separating them in existence. Being equals Energy, and Energy equals Being, just as the existence of fire equals the burning capacity of fire.

Also let us not surreptitiously smuggle into this original whole our ignorant human categories of substance and attribute, linear cause and linear effect, etc., which are applicable only to finite phenomena and limited structures of energy. In other words, it would be incorrect to think that Being is one infinite spiritual substance of which Energy is the essential attribute of power. That would immediately convert Being-Energy into an intellectual construct or imperfect conceptual formulation.*

Being-Energy as Perfection-Evolution

Having started with the all-embracing Existence-Whole which is inseparably one with the all-embracing Energy-Whole, there should be no difficulty in deriving matter, life, mind, spirit, etc. from the boundless possibilities inherent in Being-Energy via the endless process of emergent creative evolution. I have tried to show this in my book, *Being, Evolution and Immortality*.

In my view, it is not necessary to think of creative evolution in terms of *nihil fit* (out of nothing), as Henri Bergson does. Bergson felt the necessity of believing in the emergence of absolute novelties from the creative womb of Time because he wrongly equated Time with a determinate mode of Energy, i.e., *élan vital* or universal life force. Be it noted here that besides being a determinate mode of energy, Bergson's élan vital is also a conceptual abstraction insofar as no living form is ever known to exist except as the mode of behavior of a specific constellation or highly organized configuration of physico-chemical forces. Since, then, Life is a determinate mode of operation of Energy, it is not strictly infinite in the true sense of the term; so Bergson had to wave the magic wand of *ex nihilo* in order to account for the subsequent emergence of mind, intellect, and spirit from the vital impetus.

The infinite Being-Energy with which Integral Dialectics starts holds within itself boundless possibilities. Whatever novelties the evolutionary process may bring into visible form on the phenomenal level can easily be understood as determinate modes of manifestation of the "undifferentiated differences" that exist without number in the fathomless depths of Being-Energy from beginningless time.

Integral Dialectics thus gives rise to the integral philosophy of boundless Being-Energy. Infinite Energy implies the undivided unity and unbroken continuity of being and becoming, of perfection and evolution, of blissful self-existence and creative self-expression.

In order to comprehend totally the fullness of life as the multidimensional expression of Being, the philosophical method must be in the nature of a dynamic synthesis of both the ascending and the descending movements of thought. The philosophical method of Integral Dialectics must therefore represent a comprehensive and dynamic unity of both negation (*via negative,* or the Sanskrit *neti neti)* and affirmation (*via positiva* or *iti iti).*

First of all, in our search for the essential structure of the universe, we climb up the ladder (or the metaphysical mountain) of *via negativa* and keep transcending the lower levels of matter, life, mind, reason, and spirit, one after another on account of their comparative poverty of content and limitation of form. More and more clearly the light of truth begins to dawn upon our mind that Being is not just matter, or life, or mind or even spirit as known to man at a given time. Being is without a doubt infinitely richer than all these known modalities of finite existence. Then we reach a giddy height just below the top of Mount Kailasha (the towering mythological mountain of man's inner-evolutionary spiral). With ecstatic joy we behold there, at the barely visible peak, the indescribably and indeterminable Supreme Being. Although indeterminable, we realize that this Supreme Being is capable of infinite determinations, so we call it Being-Energy. We know that Energy has the ability for both descent and ascent, for creative self-expression as well as peaceful self-absorption, for spiritual reconstruction of life and society as well as the ongoing natural movement of space-time. So in perfect tune with the creative light of Being-Energy we climb down the ladder of the mystic fire *(kundalini)* again. As we climb back down we behold with great amazement that all the lower levels that we had left behind reappear now clothed in a new grandeur and invested with a new divine significance. They reveal their secret potentials for self-transformation into perfect forms of expression of the glory of Being. We spontaneously feel like saying: "This is it, This is it . . . *(iti, iti)*." This inspires us to participate in the creative flow of time with a view to manifesting more and more the boundless richness of the eternal.

Thus the dialectical movement of our thought and consciousness—the triadic rhythm of the philosophico-spiritual journey—reaches its crowning fulfillment. Our whole life becomes one overmastering passion to incarnate the eternal in time, to manifest the boundless joy of Being in the limitless flow of becoming. However, we know in our heart that no amount of manifestation can ever exhaust the inexhaustible riches of the eternal. Neither evolution nor history can ever gain victory over the vastness of Being. However much the expansiveness of time may try to take away a whole expanding universe from the infinite richness of Being, the residuum must always remain infinite.

---

*In this respect, Integral Dialectics differs from the traditional Tantric metaphysics of India. The latter starts with cosmic energy as the ultimate principle but regards it as the power of one ultimate spiritual reality, Shiva.

SCIENCE

Man's quest for unity behind plurality has been happening in science. For example, Einstein and the discovery of the unified energy field. He saw that the law of gravity explains certain phenomena. He saw that the theory of the relativity of space and time explained certain phenomena. But he was not satisfied to leave it at that, because he had a philosophical mind. This philosophical mind, this searching intelligence of man, is always looking for unity behind plurality. This is why Einstein could not rest until he caught a glimpse of some higher unity. So he began to carry on further research, and eventually made a wonderful discovery. He found that behind all these laws operative in the different realms of phenomena, it seems that there is an ultimate unity. That is what he called the unified field of energy. So, he saw that all these different laws can be explained and reduced to some more fundamental laws. This is the whole orientation of the searching mind of man. Until and unless we reach unity, we do not feel happy.

A. QUANTUM THEORY AND CONSCIOUSNESS

In our search for truth and knowledge, our mind has been splintered into so many water-tight compartments, into so many mutually exclusive disciplines of knowledge, that as a result we have lost the unified vision of the supreme truth of life. As Albert Schweitzer points out in his book *Philosophy of Civilization*,[1] the crux of the crisis of our time lies in the fact that we have lost the kind of comprehensive philosophy of life which can inspire us to deeds of courage and love. There is fragmentation of life and love, too much of it. And therein lies clearly the crisis of our civilization today. We have all kinds of dichotomies: science and mysticism are not on speaking terms with each other, we have logic and religion not on speaking terms with each other, we have ethics and politics not on speaking terms. So all these different, fragmented, splintered disciplines of knowledge, resulting in a kind of choas and confusion in the domain of consciousness. And when this happens, it is called loss of spirit. So, from that standpoint, I think that it is very important today to bring together in a harmony precious bits of information and knowledge that we have gathered over the centuries.

In our hearts all of us feel that in order to make true the dream of building one planetary culture and human civilization, to give reality to the dream of human unity, that what is of first and foremost importance is the spirit of unity in our consciousness—the image of unity in our minds. That is fundamental. In other words, of first importance is the spiritual unity which alone can lay the foundation for an interculturally, internationally unified humanity. So, this is the first point—that there is this great need for the unification of knowledge.

Some of the great thinkers of our day are doing research in this field. A lot of research is going on—now. H. G. Wells used to talk of the great need for an encyclopedia of modern knowledge. He says that the United Nations cannot do its job properly unless there is an integration of all the knowledge that man has today. So he used to talk about that encyclopedia of knowledge, of need for research in this field, bringing together all knowledge into a unified structure, a comprehensive vision of truth, of the one truth.

Dr. Oliver Reiser of the University of Pittsburg has devoted his whole life in this area—to the integration of knowledge. He has that very good book, *Integration of Knowledge*,[2] and also *Cosmic Humanism*,[3] which is about cosmic man who can emerge out of this integrated knowledge.

In the same way, in the East also, there are many great thinkers and sages who have spent their lives in this area, in the search for integrated knowledge, for the unification of all available knowledge. Sri Aurobindo comes to mind immediately. He has devoted his whole life, his research, his spiritual activity in this direction, trying to bring together all important knowledge and wisdom from different fields and disciplines, including logic and religion, science and mysticism, and politics and economics, etc., into a unified knowledge, the kind of unified knowledge that can unify humanity. The result of that effort of Aurobindo we find in his books like *Synthesis of Yoga*,[4] and *The Life Divine*,[5] the quintessence of which I have tried to express in Western terminology in my books *Integral Yoga*[6] and *Being, Evolution and Immortality*.[7]

In many areas today, in many branches of science, momentous discoveries are being made. But not all of those aware of the discoveries in modern science are aware of their revolutionary philosophical impact, or revolutionary spiritual significance—of what they imply in terms of our world picture, our overall philosophical outlook. So, I shall try to bring out for you one aspect, one important area where we find that science and spirituality have come together joining hands in affirming an indivisible truth.

One basic problem, one spiritual problem which we have all felt, which human beings have felt over the last few centuries is the disparity between the scientific view of man and the spiritual view of man. From the spiritual standpoint, man has freedom. Man is essentially a spiritual being and he has freedom. Furthermore, this freedom that man has is not an impotent kind of freedom. It is creative freedom, freedom to create new values out of the abysmal depths of his own being. That is the kind of freedom which man possesses. And this is the basic affirmation of philosophy, of religion, of mysticism. Whereas when we turn to science, we get a different picture, not only different but a diametrically opposed picture. How? Because a scientist will tell you that man, like every other thing in this world, is subject to the universal law of cause and effect, which reigns supreme in the whole universe. Which therefore means that like everything else man also is completely determined by natural forces operating according to natural laws. And these natural forces are supposed to be blind, mechanical, and thus the scientific view emerging from the law of cause and effect is that man is a creature of circumstances and forces over which he has no control.

I want you first of all to see this dichotomy here, this duality, these two radically opposite, sharply conflicting views of man. Religion, mysticism, spirituality affirm that man as a spiritual being is free, that he has freedom. So much so that he has freedom to commit sins and make mistakes. He has that much freedom. He violates laws. He has that much freedom. On the other hand, there is the scientific view according to which man is a helpless creature of circumstances beyond his control. In other words, the mechanistic view of man and the spiritualistic view of man as a free being—this is the opposition.

However, in modern science some revolutionary discoveries are being made. One such discovery is quantum mechanics. This scientific discovery now tells us that even from the standpoint of science, man has freedom. That is a discovery of epoch-making significance, revolutionary philosophical and spiritual impact, completely shaking to the foundations old-fashioned scientific knowledge. In past times, science was regulated by the atomistic viewpoint, mechanistic outlook, reductionistic attitude—that all the higher things of life such as moral, religious, mystical, spiritual phenomena can be reduced to blind forces, interaction of blind, unconscious elements of matter—atoms and molecules. That was the old-fashioned scientific outlook, summed up in this atomistic, mechanistic approach.

However, if you study and understand the discoveries of modern science, you will find that profound revolution has taken place in this outlook. The atomistic, mechanistic approach has been replaced by what is called the systems view of the universe, the organismic view of the world. This is a complete reversal of outlook, a Copernican revolution of our time. This has many implications. I shall focus my attention on one or two points especially with reference to discoveries in quantum mechanics.

Now, what is this quantum mechanics? What is new about its modern discovery? Previously, it was believed that atoms, being the ultimate constituents of this world, are all indivisible material particles, indivisible, static, inert material particles. However, the modern view is that the atom has an enormous complexity of structure. Even the simplest of atoms, the hydrogen atom, has this enormous complexity of structure, and it is a mode of expression of energy, not just inert. It is energy embodied. Every so-called passive, inert particle of matter is an embodiment of energy.

When we analyze the internal structure of the energy of an

SCIENCE 107

atom, we find there that it really resembles in its inner constituion the structure of the solar system in which we live. It is a solar system in miniature. Because just as in the solar system, the sun is in the center and the planets move, revolve around it. In the same way, when we look at the internal structure of an atom, at the center of the atom we find a positive nucleus which is the seemingly static center, and around that positive nucleus negative charges of electricity (electrons) revolve with great velocity. So this is the structure of an atom. But this is not the end of the story.

The further complexity is that the electrons have different orbits. There are different layers like in everything there are levels. Everything that exists in life has a multi-level structure, enormously complex. It has a hierarchical structure, higher and higher. In older physics, the hierarchy was not accepted. Everything was flat. But now there is another revolutionary discovery in science, the hierarchical structure of reality. Everything has a hierarchical structure. This is very evident in the human structure. This hierarchical structure has come to a very concentrated expression in man. That is why we have this erect posture expressing this hierarchy. All these energy centers are present in us, expressing the hierarchy of consciousness.

Within the constitution of an atom there is this multi-level structure. And what do we find there? It has been discovered that this little electron which revolves around the proton mysteriously enough seems to have a life of its own. It has individuality. It has freedom. So, this is what I want you to understand: that even this little electron, which is a material thing, a negative charge of electricity seems to have an intrinsic life and individuality of its own. It has freedom, baffling the calculations of the scientists who believed in the universality of causal determinism, everything is determined mechanically. The electron has defeated that theory.

The movement of the electron has demonstrated the freedom of its own to jump from one orbit to another orbit. This is very amazing that this little energy unit seems to have freedom of movement and can jump from one orbit to another orbit. This is called a quantum jump. And nobody has yet been able to figure out how this jump takes place. It cannot be figured out or calculated according to any known law of science. So you see, this opens up a whole new vista of thought: that if this freedom is possessed even by little electrons, how can we say that we human beings who stand at the apex of the ladder of evolution so far, who can dare say that we don't have freedom, that we are subject to just mechanical forces? Even a little atom is refuting that theory.

This is the first point I want to emphasize: that even from the standpoint of science and on the basis of scientific theory, in perfect harmony with known scientific knowledge, we can affirm the genuine authentic freedom of human beings. So, this can be accepted as a scientific truth. Now, the question of course would arise that if man has this freedom, or the electron has this freedom, then what about this law of causality, of cause and effect? For some time after this discovery there was some bewilderment and confusion. How can we reconcile these two things? On the one hand , we believe in the law of cause and effect and absolute determinism. On the other hand, we see there are sparks of freedom everywhere, in all the things of the world, from the minutest, infinitesimal atom to man. So, how do you reconcile these two things?

You know, many of our human problems are created by ourselves. Many of our human problems are problems of ignorance, self-created and artificially generated. So, the solution comes when that ignorance vanishes. We have created this problem when we say: how can there be both? The answer is: why not? Who tells us that there cannot be both? You see, we think that there cannot be both because we are still under the unconscious influence of the old Aristotelian law that A cannot be B *and* not B, which is another ignorance. But life is all the time knocking us out of that belief, trying to teach us a lesson that A *can* be both B and not B. The same human being for example can be both mortal and immortal. He can be determined and free. This is what the true law is. It is called the law of polarity, the law of identity of opposites, which is a new discovery again in science, psychology and philosophy today. When you come to examine the flesh and blood reality, it is a standing refutation of the old idea that A cannot be both B and not B. Everywhere in the concrete texture of reality, you will see the meeting of opposites without which nothing clicks, nothing takes place, nothing happens in life. Nothing is produced and created without the union of opposites.

Let me go back to that point where I said there can be both freedom and determinism. How do we explain that? If you are patient with me, I would like to say a few words to try to explain, to throw some light on this very important truth: the meeting of opposites.

> Reality is two in one, one is two —
> Timeless eternity and ceaseless flux of time,
> Nameless mystery and nature's creative flow.
> The two are no separate spheres of Being.
> The formless bursts forth in endless forms.
> The nameless one reveals countless names.
> The spaceless reality expands in boundless space,
> And the timeless Spirit in endless time.
> H. Chaudhuri, *The Rhythm of Truth*

Everything operates in a system. The electron is operating not by itself, but within a system, the atomic system. We are operating in the social system. Every one of us lives in a social field, in a social organism, let me say. None of us lives by himself. Everything works within a system and exercises its freedom within that system. So, both of these are there. First of all, there is freedom. But then again, that freedom is not absolute freedom. For the electron there are certain orbits, and there is an energy field of the atom. The freedom of the electron is controlled by the limitation of that system. So this freedom of movement is not absolute. It is a relative freedom. So, the electron has both freedom and also limitation or determination.

Let me now give illustrations from our human life. We are right here a system. The Cultural Integration Fellowship is a system, an organization with members of this system. So, with regard to the different members of this organization, we can say that they have freedom and also some limitation. They have some uniform pattern of behavior which they accept, but also they have their freedom, both freedom and determination. In science this is called micro-freedom with macro-determination. You see, the electron's freedom is micro-freedom, little freedom. But that freedom is circumscribed within the macro-determination of the atom as a whole, which has its own behavior pattern, which is not disturbed by the movement of the electron. That determination imposes a limit on that electron, however free it may be. In the same way, each member of Cultural Integration Fellowship has his own freedom. For example, in his political life he may be a Republican, or a Democrat, or a Socialist, or a member of the Communist Party. That is not the business of the Fellowship. Each member is free to choose his own political affiliation as well as many other things in his private life. And it is not proper for the organization to interfere in the freedom of the individual member in all the different areas of life. But then again, the organization has some uniform pattern of behavior, some constitution, some by-laws. And this is not effected by the freedom of the members in other areas. There is perfect harmony between this free movement of the individual members and also the structural idiosyncracy of the organization. To sum it up, I may say that there is no conflict between micro-freedom and macro-determination. This is how the distinction has been developed in the systems of view of modern science. In our lives, both freedom and necessity are there.

Finally, let me now develop the whole thing into a further conclusion, and that is this: when in the course of our spiritual growth, we eventually reach the glorious height of self-realization or God-realization, what happens there? What happens at that moment? We find that at that height, there is a perfect unity of opposites, of freedom and necessity. The two become one. Instead of opposites being apart and separate from each other, the more you advance in life, the more you find that opposites become one.

When, for example, you attain enlightenment, you attain the full flowering of your potential. In nirvanic vision of truth, these opposites become one in your life. On one hand, you feel necessity, you feel oneness with the spirit of the whole, with the voice of eternity, or whatever expression you care to use. That is the greatest necessity which you can experience in life, the necessity of oneness with the spirit. That becomes the major source of inspiration in your life so that you begin to think and act and live out of that tremendous inward necessity of oneness with the whole. There is no taking away from that.

This is what the German philosopher Immanuel Kant[8] called the categorical imperative of the spirit. When you hear the voice of God, that becomes the supreme necessity of your life, that becomes the categorical imperative of your life. It is an unconditional imperative of the light of truth that has dawned upon your mind. So that is necessity. But at the same time it is that very necessity which also constitutes your greatest freedom. Immediately you experience freedom. Why? Because when you become one with the divine will, or one with cosmic consciousness, you realize that is your true self, that is the Self of your self, the inmost center of your being. And therefore, to be united with that means your highest freedom because you have found the true necessity at the center of your being. When you reach the highest level of your consciousness, the two things which seem to be so different in your life now become completely one. This is what the great psychologist Carl Jung meant when he said that on a higher level of consciousness the opposites become united. You discover the real unity of opposites in life and that is your great wisdom. Now, I shall just mention another point and I shall finish.

Another point in quantum mechanics is what is called critical point. In the growth process when the critical moment arises, there is a jump, a quantum jump. This is another important thing. Suppose you put your kettle of water on the heat. It gets warmer and warmer. Up to a certain point this heating of the water doesn't produce any qualitative change. It is just getting warmer, that's all. There is no qualitative change, only quantitative change, change of degree, that's all. But then comes the critical point, the critical moment. And when the critical point comes, suddenly there is a qualitative change, transformation of quality. When water is suddenly qualitatively transformed into steam and then it hisses forth, it refuses to stay confined in that kettle any more. On the arrival of the critical point this water suddenly undergoes a metamorphosis of quality—a radical, qualitative change from one thing into another. So, water now becomes steam, and steam has an opposite characteristic of water. Water goes down and steam goes up. Suddenly at that critical moment, water is metamorphosed, which means qualitatively changed into an entirely different thing—steam. This is a miracle. It is the same kind of miracle which happens in our life, which is called a spiritual miracle. This is called conversion of consciousness.

We have been evolving and growing little by little for a

period of time. It is just quantitative change. A little more today, tomorrow you know a little more, day after tomorrow still a quantitative change. Your knowledge is quantitatively changing. In the same way, you are a little better today in your emotional tone, in your behavior pattern; maybe tomorrow a little better. These are all quantitative changes. But in the course of your inner growth and development, suddenly a critical moment arrives which is called the great psychological moment, the critical moment in the evolution of the evolving psyche. And as soon as that critical moment arrives, suddenly there is a new experience of illumination, a conversion of consciousness, a profound and moving inspiring spiritual experience, by whatever name you call it: Self-realization, God-realization, Being-realization, cosmic consciousness. What has happened is that in the course of your inner evolution, you have arrived now at a very critical moment when a qualitative change takes place within you, a radical transformation of your personality into the soaring flame of illumination, uniting you with the Supreme Being or with the Higher Self. So, this is the meaning of the saying in Buddhism that illumination or *satori* comes suddenly. But, behind this abrupt happening there is a slow continuous process of growth and evolution.

So, we understand now that just as there are quantum jumps in the atom on the part of the electron, so in the course of our development there are many quantum jumps. In meditation we experience these quantum jumps, jumps of consciousness or the unity of consciousness within you to other levels, from one level to another. In meditation you can feel these jumps. So this is really a fascinating mystery of the process of evolution. But if you understand the inner dynamics of this evolutionary process, you will no longer be confused by the fact that in the course of our development more and more of what have appeared to be opposites before become unified—opening up a whole new dimension of consciousness and experience.

B. *BRAIN RESEARCH AND INTEGRATION OF CONSCIOUSNESS*

In neurophysiology and brain research, some momentous

discoveries have been made in recent times. One astounding discovery is that man has virtually two minds. This is perfectly in harmony with his two arms, two legs, two eyes, two ears, two nostrils, etc. All action, all movement, all knowledge is the result of integrated functioning of two opposite yet cerebral organs. All this is in perfect keeping with the polarized structure of energy.

Man's two minds under the one skull are his two cerebral hemispheres or temporal lobes.[9] Each of these two hemispheres has its own highly specialized and distinguishable features and mode of functioning. This has been established on the evidence of a vast accumulation of experimental data obtained by electrical stimulation of various parts of the brain with the aid of extremely sensitive micro-electrodes.

It has been found that the left hemisphere is largely the abode of man's language ability, his distinctly human capacity for verbal communication and articulation of subtle distinctions of thought and nuances of meaning. It is the instrument of the rational, logical and analytic functions of the mind. It is specifically oriented to the world of space, time and evolution. The left brain, which controls our extroverted actions, aims at survival and self assertion. It is closely connected with such other portions of the brain as those which control the ever shifting feelings of pain and pleasure, sorrow and joy, and the impulses of fear and anger, worry and anxiety, aggression and domination. These are necessary for proper regulation of our need for adjustment in the outside world.

Closely interrelated with the left hemisphere is our right hand which is especially skillful in manipulating things of the outside world. The right hand, controlled by the left temporal lobe is the organ par excellence of the extroverted mind oriented to nature's evolutionary goals of survival, success, and conquest of space. It specializes in expressing clear-cut ideas of the intellect whether through written language or through hand gestures. It is also especially adept in gaining manual skills and in managing masterly movement and self-expression.

On the other hand, the right hemisphere has been found to be the seat of intuitive knowledge, of esthetic, religious, and mystical experience.[10] Man has intuitive apprehension of those features of reality which are not to be analyzed, but are to be grasped and appreciated in their wholeness. The right hemisphere has special proficiency in sustaining synthetic functions of the psyche, as well as transpersonal insights into the fathomless depth dimension of the timeless—the transcendental ground of the cosmic manifold. It controls our introverted movements of inward centering and upward ascending.

The right hemisphere is especially associated with the deep, sublime emotions of the heart. These include transcendental peace or non-dual peace which does not fluctuate. Pains and pleasures come with the changing circumstances of life. The right hemisphere is concerned with the unchanging reality behind the changing circumstances. It registers the unchanging emotions of unconditional love and the unconditional joy which spring spontaneously from the depths of our being.

Most people have either the left hemisphere or the right hemisphere developed. There is a disproportion. They often do not function in unison, in harmony. Such things depend upon our cultivation. If we don't do that, even though there is something very precious there, it cannot be developed. These innate faculties gradually wither away for lack of exercise and become atrophied.

It has been rightly observed that in the unfoldment of the mainstream of Western culture, it is the intellect-ruled left brain which has on the whole played a predominant role. That is why among the fruits of Western civilization are to be counted the phenomenal growth of science and technology. In the unfoldment of the mainstream of Eastern culture, on the other hand, it is the intuition-ruled right hemisphere which has on the whole played a dominant role. That is why among the treasures of the Eastern heritage are to be counted all the major religions of the world, the profundities of mystic vision, and priceless gems of original esthetic creation.

The highest cultural values of East and West can be harmonized in a higher synthesis. The emphasis in integral self-discipline is the dynamic integration of the two hemispheres. It is only through integrated functioning of both these sides that one can realize the fullness of human potential. The integrated functioning of our total being, including the synthesis of wisdom and compassion on the spiritual level, the synthesis of intellect and intuition on the mental level, and the synthesis of the right and left lobes of the brain on the physical level, are necessary for the creative wholeness of the individual man as an essential factor in the unitive wholeness of the human race.

C. *THE SCIENTIFIC METHOD*

An important methodological postulate of scientific philosophy is that you do not make any hypothesis which is not verifiable. Even if a scientist makes a hypothesis which is a working hypothesis, it must be corroborated by the facts of experience, observation, experiment. If not, it is rejected. So this is a basic method of science.

Every discipline has its own methodology, its method. One important reason why science starts with this methodological assumption is that it is the scientific method which can have a great human value, a universal human value. That is why nowadays there is a scientific humanism.

Many great scientists are in a sense, very spiritual. They have great compassion. As a matter of fact, it is some of the great scientists who are the most concerned with the crises of our present age. Because they are aware of what is happening, they have greater awareness of the crisis of the present situation, and they can be very spiritual. For example, men like Bertrand Russell, Einstein, or Oppenheimer devoted their whole lives to world peace. They had a great sense of responsibility, even though some politicians are making destructive use of their discoveries. But in their own search for truth they would not make use of the idea of God. One reason is that they want to establish something which can be accepted by everybody, which can be verified. There is no room for sentimentalism or wishful thinking. There is a danger there. As soon as you accept something on faith, I will say that my faith is different. Immediately we get into a conflict situation. So, the representatives of the different religions come to a conference, which usually ends up being a lot of discussion with smoke and heat but no light. Scientists therefore decided to follow a methodological procedure, so that when something is found to be acceptable as true, everybody can accept it. The scientific method is the method of human agreement. They will say that they don't know everything, but they shall believe in those things which are very obvious, which are irrefutable, experiential, and experimentally verified.

ONTOLOGICAL DISCIPLINE

I have found that sometimes people are very sensitive to this word discipline. By discipline, ordinarily we mean that somebody else is disciplining us. We naturally resent this because we all want to grow freely from the roots of our own being. But self-discipline is at the opposite pole from external discipline. It is disciplining ourselves in order to actualize our own potentials. . . . In the absence of discipline, we dissipate our energy. In order to accomplish something, we have to properly channel our energy. That is the meaning of self-discipline. It is the kind of discipline which leads to Being-realization.

When you develop an ontological understanding of the essential structure of the universe, knowledge is no longer separated from love and action. As you reach the higher levels of consciousness, these three become unified in experience.

A. BEING-REALIZATION

As we have tried to bring out, the natural and the spiritual interpenetrate. Right in the heart of nature the spirit dwells as its ultimate vitalizing principle and inner guidance. This was a discovery not only of the spiritual masters of the world, but this is also the truth which many modern sciences are discovering.

An insight of modern psychology as well as ancient sages is that we are in for trouble if we set up a civil war between the different aspects of our nature. The intelligent thing to do is to get to know our own nature—the basic drives, motivations, and fundamental impulses—and have a program of organized fulfillment of them. As we do so, then our psychic energy is directed along higher channels and higher values evolve.

Every phase of life has its characteristic impulses. As a person grows up, certain new impulses develop. If they are suppressed, much of one's energy will be spent in inner conflict instead of freely evolving along higher lines. By following the bent of our own psychical structure, our energy is liberated from repressive forces. There is a free flow of energy directed toward the actualization of the higher values as they emerge in our field of consciousness.

When we study the lives of creative people, we find a very interesting thing. Many of them had their inner ear open to the promptings of their psyche. As a result of this inward sensitivity, they had a sense of direction. They felt that they were being guided from within. The inner guidance is there in everyone. Often we do not pay any attention to it. It is a very small voice, and we are so conditioned that we do not pay any attention to this inner guidance. Consequently, we drift endlessly without any sense of purpose. If we do pay attention, we can have a wonderful experience of a free flow of energy focused on the fulfillment of our own individual lives, on what is called today self-actualization.

* * * * * * * * * * *

From the psychological standpoint, self-actualization is the highest ideal of personality growth. Whereas from the religious standpoint, God-realization has been the concept which has been projected as the highest goal. We find that there are some who over-emphasize self-realization and some who over-emphasize God-realization. These two ideals represent two half-truths. It is by bringing them together in a harmonious vision of the total being of man that we may develop the integral ideal of Being-realization.

Viewed from the psychological standpoint, self-actualization implies that every human being has some uniqueness of his own. For the sake of mental health and proper growth, and for a true sense of happiness and fulfillment, it is of fundamental importance that an individual become aware of his own potential and try to develop it. We all have certain talents and certain shortcomings. It is a unique combination of these different plusses and minuses which gives a distinct flavor to the psyche of every human individual.

Every human being has his own psychical makeup, his own

special character structure. And each has his own unique rhythm of growth, his law of self-development. The soul of every human being can verily be regarded as a fine flower which bursts and blossoms and ripens to maturity following the rhythm of its own being. And the ideal of self-actualization requires that we become aware of our own rhythm of self-development.

As is said in the Bhagavad Gita, "even if in pursuing your own dharma, or rhythm of being, you perish, that is far better and more glorious than trying to imitate some other person's." We often do this blissfully ignorant of the rhythm of our own being. We try to be happy by following the policy of blind imitation of somebody else's standard or pattern of development. Psychologically this is an absurdity. It can never lead us anywhere.

Let me tell you something which I used to ponder when I was very young. There was a boy whose father was a teacher very well-known and respected in society. The influence of the father had a great impact upon his young imagination, and so, in due time, he became a teacher, also. But for some reason there was a feeling of emptiness, boredom. He just could not fit himself into the teaching line. One night he had a dream. In his dream, the family guru appeared and told him, "The indigenous medical system of India has been long neglected. At present, people are so much enamored with the medicine of the West that the native therapeutic system has been neglected. I want you to revive that." That dream changed his life. By following the advice he succeeded in reviving the indigenous medical system and established pharmacies all over India.

This often happens. Individuals first of all go in a certain direction. They want to be happy and so follow some external clues and external norms and values. But one day, if one is not too alienated from his inner self, that inner guidance can be heard in the stillness of the soul.

Self-actualization is the path of fulfilling one's own potential. But this can become an incomplete ideal if one does not advance to the awareness of the ground of the self. In coming to realize the self in its fullness, one goes beyond the self. It is then that one discovers, or catches a glimpse of the ultimate ground of the self that is the sustaining medium of one's whole existence.

It sometimes happens that an individual actualizes his own

individual potential to an extent, but does not go beyond the egocentric self. One may not have any realization of God. The word God, of course, has all kinds of bad associations nowadays because different people have different ideas of God. But even though there are all these changing ideas of God, and some of these are ready to be cast into the dustbin, still there is no doubt that behind all these changing ideas there is a reality—a tremendous, fundamental reality. So perhaps a better word to express that reality is *Being*. Without Being-realization, self-realization is incomplete.

A good example of self-realization without Being-realization is the father of the concept of self-existence in Western philosophy, Frederich Nietzsche. Here is a brilliant individual, a poet and philosopher. He did achieve a degree of self-actualization, but he was very unhappy. In the latter part of his life, his unhappiness, frustration, and terrible sense of loneliness brought him to the verge of insanity. Something was lacking. He could not quite relate his achievements to humanity as a whole. He could not develop the spirit of love and compassion which spontaneously flows from authentic Being-realization. Here you see the need to go beyond the self, because the self is not the true self without its rootedness in an awareness of Being.

The fully realized self is like a lotus in full blossom. Floating on the waters, the flower is rooted deep down below the water in the mud. It has grown and blossomed in the light of the sun. In the same way, the human soul is rooted in the depths of the unconscious. Our conscious self is only a fragment of our total being. It strikes its roots deep down below in the depths of the unconscious. We cannot, therefore, achieve self-actualization without incorporating all the different forces of the unconscious into the concrete texture of our personality. But that is not all. The self is also what it is in response to the light of the superconscious. The self cannot be fully actualized without the discovery of the infinite light of Being-realization. Our life becomes completely integrated only as a result of our awareness of the reality of the super-conscient.

When one transcends the boundaries of the mind and the conceptual understanding, and steps forth into Being, the first experience is tremendous and overwhelming. It is difficult to take unless one is thoroughly trained—physically, mentally, intellectually, ethically. A great deal of training is necessary to bear the impact of immediate Being-realization. As Rudolph Otto in his book, *The Idea of the Holy*,[1] points out, direct experience of the supreme reality is the experience of *mysterium tremendum*. It is unprecedented. One cannot think of any analogue in previous experience. It outsoars all logical conceptions and philosophical categories.

What is the view of the self when we have this experience? Some have used the analogy of the vast, boundless ocean. When you enter into this realm of Being-realization, first of all you are impressed profoundly with the unfathomable mystery of the all-encompassing nature of it. And then you experience yourself as a wave rolling on the ocean of consciousness. Or you may feel yourself as a spark emanating from the cosmic flame. Or we can use the scientific analogy and say that Being is the vast space-time continuum and we are like the different configurations of energy rising from the depths of that, abiding for awhile, and getting dissolved again.

A very interesting feature of this experience is that a profound change takes place in your personality. Just as on the one hand it is a very tremendous experience, on the other it is a dynamic experience; nobody can sit quiet. It is so inspiring that you are reborn with a new sense of purpose and a new self-image. True wisdom lies in the experience of this basic truth of lfe—the uninterrupted wholeness of Being.

B. *MEDITATION FOR INTEGRAL SELF-DEVELOPMENT*

A person can be an intellectual giant—he may have encyclopedic knowledge about different things of the world—but still it may not transform his whole being. There may be quite a gulf between what he is thinking and what he is doing from day to day. Meditation is an affair of one's total being. The aim of meditation is existential encounter with the ground of all being.

The distinction between prayer and meditation has been neatly expressed in this way—in prayer we talk to God, in meditation we allow God to talk to us. In prayer our mind is full of its own desires which we place before the image of God. In meditation we try to bring this chattering mind of ours to a stop and try to establish silence in our mind. We try to get into a mood of receptivity, a mood of self-opening to the light and power of higher consciousness. The indwelling light of truth has a chance to shine out and the voice of Being has a chance to articulate itself, to utter forth in the depth of silence of our being.

Very often the question is brought up—Is meditation a kind of auto-suggestion or self-hypnosis? Let me say that suggestion plays a very important role in our society, in some form or other. There is no getting away from it. As a matter of fact, the whole scheme of education in many countries is based upon the power of suggestion. All the time, from different directions, ideas are being suggested to your mind, especially today, thanks to mass media. So much of this is a kind of sociocultural conditioning. It is not necessarily bad, but it is very powerful and can have harmful effects on us.

In that context, I would like to tell you what meditation is. There is an element of suggestion here, too. But the basic principle here is to remove the effects of a wrong suggestion with the help of a better suggestion. And then you have to go beyond both.

There are all kinds of images of man. Whereas some say that man is sinful, animalistic, or nothing more than a complicated machine, others say that man is essentially a spark of the Divine. The way we live, the way we act, the way we deal with our fellow beings, is unconsciously determined by the concept of our own self—the image of man that we have accepted. In meditation we concentrate upon the true essence of our being.

Ultimately, only that is real in our life which we experience. Concrete, living experience is the touchstone of reality. So long as we have no experience of higher consciousness, it is just a sentiment, a mere hypothesis, a secondhand concept. This is why the great spiritual masters did not talk very much. They wanted to show people the way, which by following, they could have some kind of experience which would convince them of the reality of higher powers and levels of consciousness. Buddha, for example, had many people come to him—scholars, theologians, philosophers—who wanted to drag him into a discussion regarding the nature of ultimate reality. He answered all these with silence. He was not interested in metaphysical discussion about ultimate reality. He was interested in showing people the way, which by following, they would experience it. That is the only practical way. Otherwise, whatever a person may tell you, even though you may feel exhalted for a while, everything will fade away if you have no experience. So, meditation is therefore the technique of attaining some experience, real, authentic, concrete experience of the ultimate reality.

*   *   *   *   *   *   *   *

What I consider to be the best kind of meditation is creative meditation. It is meditation for integral self-development and balanced growth of personality, both empirical and transcendental. There are three essential characteristics of creative meditation.

One feature is activity, or dynamizing the creative energies of the soul. In every one of us there are some creative potentialities. In every human soul there is a latent divinity. That is to say, some profound creative energy. The fundamental spiritual task of life is to dynamize these latent energies. Meditation can help us in doing so.

The second characteristic feature is attaining what I may call dynamic union with Being. Throughout the history of Man's spiritual effort, we find that there have been two ideas which have animated him. One, the ideal of static union with God, is union with Being on a transcendental plane and attaining eternal peace and rest. Another is the dynamic ideal, not only being united with Being, but also consciously cooperating in the fulfillment of the cosmic plan of evolutionary nature.

When we understand this, another thing follows. Another feature of creative meditation is what I may call transformation. If your goal is dynamic union with Being in the sphere of human relations and social transactions, then your entire being becomes very precious. Your body, your sense, your intellect, your "I-sense", even the unconscious impulses, instinctual drives—all these become important. These are the means of action. Your job, from the spiritual standpoint, is not to starve them, is not to mortify them, but to transform them, to bring out their latent divinity.

In practicing creative meditation, first of all we have to have a clear conception of the goal. As you know, in every sphere of activity, in every effort, the first essential is to have a clear conception of where you are going. If you don't have a clear conception of your aim, then there is sure to be disorder, malfunctioning. So, this is the first essential. The goal of creative meditation is the transformation of our total personality in the light of higher consciousness.

The inmost secret of creative meditation is silent self-opening to the higher consciousness. Very often in our spiritual practices we surround ourselves with all kinds of noises. We have a tendency to depend upon external crutches. We can even be too dependent upon external music, chanting, singing. Instead of entering into the silence of our being, we may allow the mind to be carried off by these external things. This has its value, of course, but in creative meditation the secret is silence. The first important thing is to be as quiet as possible and to establish as much silence as possible on all stratas of your being.

As you establish and practice silence, you open your inner consciousness, your inner heart, without any reservation. You open your heart to the light of the Supreme, telling yourself during this period of meditation that you are not going to do anything. You are not going to press any wishes or desires, but you are opening your heart to the divine will. That should be the attitude. This is how the hidden springs of creativity can be opened. It is by practicing this silent self-opening that you can enter into fruitful communion, or communication, with the inner depths of your personality, the depths of your being.

Each one of us has a depth dimension. It remains closed most of our life because we don't pay any attention. We are too busy fulfilling our own superficial wishes and desires. We can dynamize, activate this depth dimension and enter into fruitful communion with the deeper realms of our consciousness by practicing this silent self-opening. When there is self-opening, there comes a need for concentration on Being. The all-inclusive Being is the medium in which we live and move and have our existence.

Let me give some illustrations to show how this is done in the different spheres of life:

An artist can express himself artistically and by creative imagination can enter into the spirit of nature. A landscape painter, for example, will go into the heart of nature. He observes the landscape in all its detail and concrete fullness, in all its beauty and charm and sublimity. In that way he gets absorbed in the atmosphere of nature. Having done this observing, then he meditates. He enters into the silence of his being. He allows the spirit of nature to animate him from within. No great work can be created without inner inspiration. So, he meditates and then allows the spirit of nature to be revealed within him. He feels a oneness with the landscape, and that is the moment for creation.

When there is this exhalted sense of oneness with the spirit of nature, that is the moment of self-expression. At that moment he can truly say that he is not painting that landscape, the landscape is painting itself through him. Whether it is painting or writing a poem or whatever it is, this is it—this is creative self-expression. This creative self-expression flows from an inward sense of oneness with the spirit, in this case with the spirit of nature.

Let us take the case of a businessman meditating creatively. Some people will say, "What business has a businessman to be meditating? If he wants to meditate, he must give up his business." But from the standpoint of integral self-development, every sphere of activity can be very important. No area of life, no sphere of activity, no avocation, is of negligible value; each has its importance. People in all spheres of life can follow the spiritual ideal without giving up their activities. That is to say that people in all avocations can follow a spiritual ideal and meditate. The goal is to transform one's sphere of action into a means of fulfilling the divine will, or acting as a focus of Being. So, even business activity can become part of meditation, spiritual advancement, because all these things depend upon one's attitude.

Therefore, in order for a businessman to meditate and develop spiritually, first of all there has to be the right understanding. It is not necessary for him to think that when he is doing business it has nothing to do with meditation. This would be a divisive, compartmentalized view of life, which can have very tragic and disastrous consequences for healthy growth. The important idea is more and more to transform all actions into an avenue for expressing the glory of Being. So, the principle of self-offering, again, silent self-opening and self-offering, concentrating on the divine will as the ultimate motivating factor in life is desirable.

Let us take the case of the student. His focus of attention is upon learning, study. How can he practice self-opening in carrying on his studies? Even study can become part of meditation. In reading a book there are many techniques to remember. The first important thing is objective thinking— an attempt to understand objectively what the book is trying to say. Many people don't have that ability. As they go through a book, before they get the author's idea, their own ideas are projected into the book. So often I have seen this happen. There is need for training in objective thinking. So here again—self-opening.

Having read a book and having set it aside, you may refer the whole matter to your inner self. With regard to that particular subject, see what your inner being has to say. If you learn to refer the whole matter to your inner self, seeking from within what light can come and what ideas you may have on the subject yourself.

So regardless of your avocation—artist, businessman, or student, every human being can practice meditation for his inner spiritual growth. From the practical standpoint, the most important feature is the discovery and understanding of the divine purpose and destiny of your life. This releases the creative energies of your soul toward the fulfillment of this felt will of the infinite Being.

Supramental Meditation

At the end of every age, when we study history we find this, old gods die and men search for new. This is a characteristic of transitional periods. In the present age we find that there is a search for new values. As clear as anything, they are in the process of being born in human consciousness. When men go through such a transition period they are reborn in a new kind of consciousness which lays the foundation for a new pattern of living. In spite of the fact that many problems have come to the fore today, we find as a reaction to the impact of these problems that there is a gradual awakening of a new kind of consciousness. It foreshadows the shape of things to come. Supramental meditation is a kind of self-preparation for participation in the advent of the new age—to be illuminated and transformed by the light of this newly emerging consciousness. It is not for those who go to meditation as an escape from reality. It is not for those who are just searching for personal peace, success, or aggrandizement. It is also not for those who are searching for quick results, for some kind of magic power, or instant bliss.

Supramental meditation is for those who are really willing to dedicate their lives to the divine will. It can be meaningful only to those who are not concerned only with their own personal happiness or pleasure, but who have a broader global perspective, who have some inkling of the meaning of history, the meaning of the march of civilization, the meaning of what is happening of the global scale.

When I say total self-giving, I want to emphasize that meditation is not something that you practice only for half an hour or an hour a day. That is a piecemeal, isolationist view of meditation. Many people think that you set aside a few minutes and you do it, and after you are through, you are through. Then you jump off into your normal activities of the day in a different orientation, a different spirit, no matter what you did during the period of meditation. Truly speaking, meditation is intended to give you a whole new lifestyle—living in tune with the infinite in all the details of your daily activities.

Meditation is not just a technique, a device; that can be a terminological trap. It is a way of living in tune with the infinite, in total dedication to the divine will. And so, the whole idea of setting aside a portion of your time for intensive meditation is to develop that spirit, so that you can apply it to the rest of your life. This is what I mean by total self-giving.

Here is how you can go about the practice of meditation from the supramental standpoint. Relax and let go of your mind and body. Take a few deep breaths. Say your favorite mantra a few times, and then close your eyes. Make a resolve of putting yourself heart and soul into the hands of Being. Just be humble. Since you do not know exactly what the divine will for you is at this moment, just accept that and have a complete humility of spirit, and completely give yourself into the hands of the divine. Let the divine light or the divine power meditate for you. That is when real meditation begins.

Total self-giving is not only on the intellectual or emotional level, but on all the levels of your being. Sometimes it happens that we give up a portion of our being, but we have some instinctual habits to which we cling with tenacity. If you really understand and practice total self-giving, you have to open all the different chambers of your inner existence to the light and power and love of Being. That is only when the divine has the opportunity to be manifest and to operate within your life.

The human mind being as it is, it is only natural that it will be wandering, especially in the initial stages. Just for a few minutes maybe, you hold fast in this spirit of self-giving, but pretty soon you forget. There is a rush of ideas and images into your mind. All those who have tried to meditate would testify that this is a great problem—the problem of the wandering mind, what the ancient sages called the monkey mind. The mind is like a monkey which is always jumping around. You cannot hold to one thing for any length of time. As soon as you have succeeded in holding it to a particular idea for a few minutes, unexpectedly it is gone somewhere else. So, what do you do?

Whatever ideas may come, don't feel disturbed. You have to know that this is the natural tendency of the mind. Don't immediately take up arms against it in an attitude of fighting it. This fighting attitude is self-defeating. As soon as you give up the fighting attitude, and you have a relaxed attitude of acceptance, your enemy is disarmed. As other irrelevant ideas, images, impulses, wishes rushing from the depths of your unconscious psyche appear in your mental vision, in the foreground of your consciousness, just calmly look at them. Take note of them. Observe them in a very calm, dispassionate way. And then as you take note of them, offer them to the divine.

Here you are practicing self-giving. All these things are part of your being. And as I said, self-giving must be total. This act of offering is a wonderful technique, if I may use that term here. What happens is that as you observe and offer them to the divine, you disidentify, you detach from them. Then, you expose them to the light and power of divine consciousness so that they are melted there.

Another principle is total use of a mantra. You are of course familiar with the word mantra—a spiritual sound, a spiritual formula, for example, "Om" is a mantra which expresses the wholeness of Being, or "Om, shanti, shanti, shanti" (peace that passeth understanding) is a mantra. There are all kinds of mantras. There are some sounds which have a rhythmically powerful effect upon your mind and body, but may not have any meaning, may not appeal to your intellect. But by virtue of the fact that it is a powerful mantra, a rhythmical constellation of sound vibrations, it can have some powerful effects upon you. This is a nonconnotative mantra. Zen Buddhists use that, and Maharishi Mahesh Yogi has used non-connotative mantras.

In using a non-connotative mantra, you are getting some results, but you are not using the full potential of the mantra. The mantra has three-fold power. One is the sound vibration, which may evoke some visual image, also. For example, when you say "Om, shiva, shakti" it means cosmic energy-consciousness. If you are instructed in that way, then it will evoke the image of a vast, boundless ocean. So, immediately as you are saying the mantra, you are hearing the sound and you are visualizing the vast, boundless ocean, which is the ocean of cosmic energy. You are making a double use of the mantra here, a sound effect and a visual image.

Another power of the mantra is its ideological implication. Man is after all a thinking being. So, all the different aspects of his being have to be engaged, have to be involved in the spiritual search. In other words, if you use the mantra in such a way that you can relate to this mantra with your capacity for sound, your capacity for vision, and your capacity for thinking—if you use the mantra in this full measure, then you are advancing with the power of your whole being.

Finally, another basic principle of supramental meditation is what is called the dialectical movement of consciousness. Dialectical here means the dynamic unity of opposites. In other words, in the full practice of meditation, there is a twin movement of your consciousness—ascent followed by descent, or ingoing followed by outgoing, or introversion followed by extroversion. In this way you complete the circle.

As you go deeper into meditation, you feel like going deeper and deeper within yourself towards the inmost center of your being, or you may feel like rising higher and higher up in the hierarchy of consciousness. This is the ascending movement of consciousness. Many traditional mystics or spiritual seekers have been satisfied with this one movement. But in supramental meditation, this must be followed by the opposite movement of consciousness, so that there is established in your mind, in your inner consciousness, the dynamic unity of these opposites. It is always out of the dynamic union of opposites that wonderful things are born.

As you ascend, you remember that it is not your goal simply to be united with the divine. It is your goal to manifest the divine glory in life and society and human relations. Remembering that, you come down armed with some of the power and light and love and joy of the divine into your being, so that you can radiate a more illuminated consciousness. This is what I mean by dialectical movement of consciousness—ascent followed by descent. You may feel like going within and reaching the inmost center of your being, but the center is nothing without the circumference. So, you reach the center, but you don't stay there and become a hermit. Introversion must be followed by extraversion. Having reached the center and contacted the peace and joy of the divine, then you come out with that powerful light. Here your whole personality becomes an image of Being, with a view to establishing something of the divine glory in society.

EPILOGUE

In the history of human civilization we find that unitive consciousness so far has been manifest only in very isolated individuals, like Christ, Buddha, Krishna, Lao Tsu, Zoroaster, Moses—they had some of this unitive consciousness. In the process of evolution, the next big step may be that this unitive or integral consciousness will be operative in the collective mind of man, in the collective life of humanity.

A. *THE FUTURE OF CIVILIZATION*

In discussing the future of man, or the future of civilization, the question arises—Why think of the future at all? Why not just be satisfied with the present moment? Well, that is good and valid for those who are not strong enough to take life in their own hands and prepare for the future to make something meaningful out of their life. But regarding those who are healthy, who are dynamic, a forward-looking vision of the future is very important because man is essentially a forward-looking creature. As Teilhard de Chardin has pointed out, the human mind is like an arrow pointing to the future. All the great things that man has been able to build and all the progress that he has been able to achieve in the different fields can be traced to this characteristic.

It is the prerogative of man more and more to actualize the inherent potentials of his being. This is why the vision of the future is important. We have to become aware of our potential. We have to project our vision into the future toward an ideal for which we can strive. And exactly to that extent our life becomes meaningful.

The scientist-philosopher, Korzybski, says in his book *Science and Sanity*,[1] that man is a time-binding creature. This means that he can look back and take note of his past experiences and situations—failures and successes—and profit from them. Having extracted the lessons of the past, he has to let the past bury itself. He now projects his vision into the future: "What is it that I want in life? What is the goal of my existence?" After he makes clear in his mind where he is going, then he is in a position to concentrate his energy on the things to be done in the present. In this way, his present may creatively advance into the future. This is time-binding, binding the past, the present, and the future; his whole life becomes, therefore, extended in time. It is a creative and dynamic flow from the past to the present toward the future.

When we look to the future, we find that different people as they survey the happenings around the globe react to them in different ways. There are some who, taking note of the distressing features of this world, become very pessimistic. Then again, there are some who are buoyantly optimistic. And then, of course, there are some who steer the middle course, who develop what we may call a realistic, cautious type of optimism. I would like to discuss briefly these three different attitudes.

Depending upon many factors which are closely relevant to our personal life—bank balance, social adjustment, harmony with the environment, and one's own physical condition—these factors determine how one looks at the world. If there are depressing factors in one's own life situation, he focuses upon the depressive happenings of life. But if he has resilience of the spirit within, due to psychic integration and inner balance, he notices the encouraging signs of the times.

As we look around, of course, we find that there are many depressing things. There are several brushfires around the globe. We get the feeling that mankind is sitting on the edge of a volcano. We never know when there is going to be a terrific volcanic eruption. This is certainly frightening. It is especially frightening today because of the fact that the whole of mankind has become one entity. All problems today are world problems. We can no longer think in terms of a world half peaceful and half in war—it's just not possible.

We have to visualize the different trends. We have to think about what is likely to happen twenty years from now, twenty-five years from now, and prepare for that eventuality. Otherwise, with the rapid pace at which things are changing, the future will be delivering ruder and ruder shocks to us, and we will pretty soon be caught in a situation for which we are not prepared at all.

Those who are overly pessimistic look and concentrate on the dark side. But we must not forget that there is a silver lining to the darkest cloud. We have to understand the significance of the bright features and potentials. From the very beginning of civilization, we find that there have been prophets of doom who have been predicting that the end of the world is at hand and that the whole of mankind is going to be destroyed.

On the other side of the picture, there are optimists. There are some who carry optimism to an extreme. They become over-optimistic, unrealistically optimistic. To give you an analysis of the reasons of this, there are some who have a kind of inner feeling that if they look the other way, their problems will disappear. If they don't see the problems, then they don't exist. There are some who can afford to be very optimistic following this principle. Others become optimistic in a selfish kind of way. They themselves may be very fortunately positioned in life and they take the attitude—'after me, the deluge.' Then there are some who become very optimistic because of their belief that no matter how dark and dismal things may appear to be, there is a great God up there and everything will be set right. Sometimes this becomes very sentimental. As a psychologist would say, this can be traced to a very childish attitude. Just as a little child, whatever the problem may be, feels that if he cries, Mama will come running along and will set things right again. Some people carry this attitude all of their lives.

Having discussed these extreme positions, I would like to say a word about a healthy, balanced, optimistic outlook on life. I personally believe in optimism. This very attitude of optimism is good because by being an optimist, by looking forward to the future with hope and with self-confidence, we generate positive forces. By adopting this outlook, we immediately put ourselves in dynamic contact with the boundless reservoir of energy that is characteristic of Being.

Setting aside all ethical considerations, if we just look to the psychological and biological constitution of man, we find that there is reason to be optimistic. As you may know, there are two fundamental instincts in man. One is the instinct of survival—the will to live. And the other is the death impulse. Most of the tragic happenings of life ultimately are traceable to the death impulse. All the destruction that is going on is ultimately traceable to this impulse. But even though there is this death impulse, the will to live is more powerful. The instinct of survival is the most powerful instinct in man. That is why in a country, for example, different people, different parties may be squabbling with each other, but when the country is confronted with a common danger all the parties sink their differences and join hands together. Why? The instinct of survival, the will to live, is more powerful than the destructive impulse. So, this is the basic reason to be optimistic.

Today we are beginning to see that all nations are beginning to realize the magnitude of world problems. Many problems cannot be solved by any one nation. All nations have to put their heads together. I was reading an article the other day that even diametrically opposed political entities are co-operating in a transnational agency, a global weather bureau which is keeping tabs on the weather all over the world. This sort of thing is very interesting.

Thanks to a worldwide network of communication and transportation, the world has become very small and we have naturally begun to develop a global awareness. But recently we have passed from global perspective to cosmic perspective. After man's landing on the moon, revolutionary change in man's self-awareness is change in the direction of cosmic perspective. We are realizing more and more how this human race with its very unique and precious heritage belongs to one tiny speck of dust which occupies a small corner of the intergalactic system. That has given tremendous urgency to the problems of human survival. It is a factor which is going to unify, which is going to enable different peoples to sink their differences and join hands together to lick the problems with concerted effort.

I remember during the last great world war when things were in a terrible mess, some people wrote to Sri Aurobindo. He had an optimistic outlook which was based upon his survey of the process of human evolution. They wrote to him, "What do you think? The world seems to be in a big mess, do you still maintain your optimism?" He very briefly answered, "You must remember that the night is darkest before the dawn, but the dawn is sure to come." This statement is based upon his view of evolution. In the process of evolution there is a cyclical order. Once in a while, in accordance with the very method of nature, the inherent contradictions of life come to the front. This is the situation today.

We are going through a transitional period of evolution, of terrestrial evolution. In this period of transition and transitional crisis, all the latent contradictions and discrepancies of human nature have come to the foreground of our consciousness resulting in a very chaotic situation. But it is the strategy of nature that as these things come to the front, as our problems come out in all their nakedness, we have a chance to understand them, come to grips with them, and to do something about them.

Finally, I should like to mention one thing and conclude. The problems that we see today, the problems of division and separation, the problems of conflict and crisis, are ultimately traceable to the level of consciousness on which we are functioning. But just as in the course of evolution the rational mind of man evolved out of the matrix of the sentient consciousness of the animal, another breakthrough in evolution is coming when out of the rational consciousness of man a higher type of consciousness is going to emerge. This is what we have called an integral consciousness. It is in the cards that this type of consciousness will be operative in the collective life of humanity. This will eventually give rise to an entirely new order of civilization, a unique world order of real unity, peace, harmony, and progress.

B. *NOTES ON THE INFLUENCE OF SRI AUROBINDO*

Sri Aurobinko ranks among the world's foremost mystic seers, poets and philosophers. As a spiritual leader he was amazingly dynamic. As a speculative thinker he was profoundly creative. He has given the world a very comprehensive philosophical system, a new spiritual synthesis, an inspiring *weltanshauung*. But what is more important, he has also given to the world a complete art of integral living. It points the way to dynamic integration of the material and spiritual values of life. It is a call to the reconstruction of human life and society on the basis of abiding spiritual values.

* * *

My first inspiration came from the writings of Vivekananda and Ramakrishna, who were both from Bengal as was I. Later on, I discovered Sri Aurobindo and my interest in him actually goes back to 1935.

I was on the faculty of a city college in Calcutta teaching philosophy and doing research in comparative philosophy East and West. I wrote to Aurobindo before I made my trip to his ashram in Pondicherry about the purpose of my visit—my interest in philosophical thinking and research. At that time, I was a little bit sceptical about religion and mysticism. I had a feeling that it was kind of dreamy stuff, although I did believe in moral values. So, I went there with a sceptical attitude.

I was going through the motion of participating in the different meditation groups, but I was not really meditating. While everybody else was seriously in meditation, closing their eyes, I was all observation with my eyes open. After a few days, however, I thought that I would give it a try. And you know, I had a very strange, overwhelming experience. That was the first time in my life that I understood the true meaning of meditation. That was a turning point in my life.

REFERENCES AND NOTES

PHILOSOPHY

1 Karl Jaspers, *Way to Wisdom* (New Haven: Yale University Press, 1954), pp. 30-31.

2 Martin Heidegger, *Existence and Being* (Chicago: Henry Regnery Company, 1949), p. 389.

3 Samuel Alexander, *Space, Time and Deity,* 2 vols. (London: Macmillan & Co., 1927).

4 Pierre Teilhard de Chardin, *The Phenomenon of Man* (New York: Harper & Bros., 1959).

5 Martin Heidegger, *Existence and Being* (Chicago: Henry Regnery Co., 1949), p. 35.

6 W. T. Stace, *The Philosophy of Hegel* (New York: Dover Publications, 1955), p. 87.

7 *Ibid.,* p. 136.

8 Vincent Vyacinas, *Earth and Gods: An Introduction to the Philosophy of Martin Heidegger* (The Hague: Martinus Nijhoff, 1961), p. 106.

9 Taittiriya Upanishad, 111.1.1.

10 *Ibid.,* 111.2.1.

11 Tyndall's Belfast Address of 1874. Quoted in H. Seth Pringle Pattison, *The Idea of God* (New York: Oxford University Press, 1920), p. 105.

12 *Taittiriya Upanishad,* 111.2.1.

13 *Ibid.,* 111.4.1.

14 *Ibid.,* 111.5.1.

15 *Ibid.,* 111.6.1.

16 Pierre Teilhard de Chardin, *The Phenomenon of Man* (New York: Harper, 1959), pp. 56, 57, 72.

17 *Ibid.,* p. 308.

18 Sri Aurobindo, *The Life Divine* (New York: Sri Aurobindo Library, 1951), p. 276.

19 Edmund Husserl, *Ideas: General Introduction of Pure Phenomenology* (London: Allen & Unwin, 1958), pp. 242-243.

20 Jean-Paul Sartre, *The Transcendence of the Ego* (New York: Noonday, 1959), pp. 44-45.

138   REFERENCES AND NOTES

21 Samuel Alexander, *Space, Time and Deity* (London: Macmillan, 1934), II, 82.

22 Sartre, *Transcendence of Ego*, p. 48: "There is no I on the un-reflected level." *See also* pp. 80-81: "The ego is an object appre-hended, but also an object constituted by reflective con-sciousness."

23 J. R. Ballantyne trans., *Samkhya Aphorisms of Kapila* (Varanasi: Chowkhamba Sanskrit Series Office, 1963), p. 455. *See also* Chat-terjee and Datta, *An Introduction to Indian Philosophy* (Calcutta: University of Calcutta, 1950), p. 269: "The self is not a substance with the *attribute* of consciousness, but it is pure consciousness as such."

24 S. Radhakrishnan, *Indian Philosophy* (London: Allen and Unwin, 1958), II. 283.

25 Chatterjee and Datta, *Introduction to Indian Philosophy*, p. 286.

26 Sartre, *Transcendence of Ego*, p. 28.

27 *Ibid.*, p. 93.

HISTORY

1 Oswald Spengler, *The Decline of the West* (New York: Knopf, 1962).

2 *Ibid.*, p. 18.

3 Pierre Teilhard de Chardin, *The Phenomenon of Man* (New York: Harper & Bros., 1959), pp. 14-15.

4 Grace Cairns, *Philosophies of History* (New York: Philosophical Library, 1962).

5 *Ibid.*

6 Arnold Toynbee, *Civilization on Trial* (New York: Oxford Uni-versity Press, 1948).

PSYCHOLOGY

1 James R. Ballantyne, trans., *The Samkhya Aphorisms of Kapili* (Varanasi: Chow Khamba Sanskrit Series Office, 1963), p. 270.

2 Sri Aurobindo, *The Life Divine* (New York: E. P. Dutton & Co., 1953), p. 78.

3 Frederick Nietzsche, *Thus Spake Zarathustra* (Baltimore: Penguin Books, 1966), p. 54.

4 Abraham Maslow, *Toward A Psychology of Being* (Princeton, N.J.: D. Van Nostrand Co., 1962), pp. 25, 33, 39.

5 Sri Aurobindo, *Thoughts and Glimpses* (Pondicherry, India: Sri Aurobindo Ashram, 1964), p. 3.

6 William James, *Varieties of Religious Experience* (New York: New American Library, 1958).

EDUCATION

1 Carl Jung, *The Undiscovered Self* (New York: Little, Brown, & Co. 1957).

2 R. D. Laing, *The Divided Self* (New York: Pantheon, 1969).

3 Aldous Huxley, *The Perennial Philosophy* (New York: Harper & Bros. 1945).

METHODOLOGY

1 S. Radhakrishnan, *The Principal Upanishads* (New York: Harper & Bros., 1953), pp. 164-65.

2 Johnston & Struthers, trans., *Hegel's Science of Logic*, Vol. 1 (London: George Allen & Unwin, 1929), p. 94.

3 H. Bhattacharya, ed., *The Cultural Heritage of India*, Vol. 111 (Calcutta: Ramakrishna Mission Institute of Indian Culture, 1953), p. 240.

4 Frank Thilly, *A History of Philosophy* (New York: Henry Holt & Co., 1936), pp. 296-297.

SCIENCE

1 Albert Schweitzer, *The Philosophy of Civilization* (Atlantic Highlands, N.J.: Humanities Press, 1971).

2 Oliver Reiser, *Integration of Human Knowledge* (Boston: Porter Sargent, 1958).

3 _____, *Cosmic Humanism* (Cambridge, Mass.: Schenkman Publishing Co., 1966).

4 Sri Aurobindo, *Synthesis of Yoga* (Pondicherry, India: Sri Aurobindo Ashram, 1959).

5 _____, *The Life Divine* (New York: E. P. Dutton, 1953).

6 Haridas Chaudhuri, *Integral Yoga* (Wheaton: Theosophical Publighing House, 1965).

7 _____, *Being, Evolution, & Immortality* (Wheaton: Theosophical Publishing House, 1974).

8 Immanuel Kant, (New York: Dolphin, 1961).

9 Nigel Calder, *The Mind of Man* (New York: Viking Press, 1970), pp. 243-263.

10 Robert Ornstein, *The Psychology of Consciousness* (San Francisco: W. H. Freeman, 1972), pp. 8-13.

ONTOLOGICAL DISCIPLINE

1 Rudolph Otto, *The Idea of the Holy* (New York: Oxford University Press, 1950).

EPILOGUE

1 Alfred Korzybski, *Science and Sanity* (Lakeville, Connecticut: International Non-Aristotelian Library, 1958).

RECOMMENDED READING

Harman, Willis. *Incomplete Guide to the Future*. Stanford, California: Stanford Alumni Association, 1976.